DATE DUE

NOV 4 1997	
GAYLORD	PRINTED IN U.S.A.

SOCIAL WORK
An Outline for the Intending Student

SOCIAL WORK
An Outline for the Intending Student

by
Noel Timms
*(Professor of Applied Social Studies,
Bradford University)*

LONDON
ROUTLEDGE & KEGAN PAUL

First published 1970
by Routledge & Kegan Paul Ltd
Broadway House, 68–74 Carter Lane
London EC4V 5EL

Reprinted 1973

Printed in Great Britain by
Redwood Press Limited
Trowbridge, Wiltshire

ISBN 0 7100 6789 5 (c)
ISBN 0 7100 6790 9 (p)

CONTENTS

I

Introduction: Some Historical Considerations

THIS BOOK IS NOT a manual of practice: it is an attempt to introduce students and others who wish to learn about social work to the broad dimensions of the subject. It will be successful if the reader becomes acquainted with the methods social workers use, the knowledge they require in order to work effectively, the values they espouse, the organizations within which they work, and the ways in which they are trained. Chapters will be devoted to each of these subjects, but the objective will not be an exhaustive inventory of all necessary items. The space devoted to each topic varies considerably and should not be assumed to represent any precise valuation of the place the topic occupies in the over-all activity of social work. The aim is to introduce questions which appear to be both interesting and crucial. Thus, references to the history of social work in the present chapter will not rehearse the familiar and misleading story of developments from the time of Christ ('the first social worker'), down to the present century, with brief stops in the sixteenth century and a longer pause in the nineteenth. We shall be concerned instead with raising questions about the plausibility of existing accounts and the possibility of a genuine historical approach to the development of social work. Throughout the present book social work will be treated as a subject worth sustained intellectual activity, as a topic that rewards imaginative curiosity.

This kind of approach is relatively unusual and may disappoint some in search of an introduction to the subject. Social workers do not usually enjoy a reputation for sustained critical thought about what they do. They are seen characteristically in feminine terms, as high-souled, low-heeled women somewhat anxious to intervene in the lives of others. Their activities are often considered praiseworthy, but not very remarkable or puzzling. They are assumed to raise few questions of interest except to those practising, or those who seek to benefit from, social work. Many would apply to the contemporary social worker Emerson's comment on philanthropists in the last century: 'I go to a convention of philanthropists. Do what I can, I cannot keep my eyes off the clock.' This book questions the inevitability of the boredom implicit in Emerson's remark and aims to discuss some of the issues in social work that are of general interest. Such discussion may appear to be simply a way of avoiding getting down to the business of helping individuals or of reconstructing society so that the problems with which social workers deal can be abolished. Others may feel that the approach adopted in this book camouflages the essential fact that social work is primarily a question of practical aid and the essentially incommunicable and spontaneous relationships between social workers and those they would help. These viewpoints contain some important arguments about the nature of social work, but they cannot be accepted as satisfactory starting points for an introduction to social work that claims some adequacy. It is impossible to assess arguments of this kind until one has gained some familiarity with the world of social work.

It might be expected that an introduction to a subject would begin with a succinct definition. There is no shortage of definitions, but few, if any, are informative. Sometimes the definitions are much too wide, so that people are included in the category of social worker who do not really look as if they belong. On occasions the category seems to include everyone. Thus, Devine[1] dedicated his book *The Spirit of Social Work* to

> social workers, that is to say, to every man and woman, who, in any relation of life, professional, industrial, political, educational or domestic; whether on salary or as a

volunteer; whether on his own individual account or as part of an organized movement, is working consciously, according to his light intelligently, and according to his strength persistently, for the promotion of the common welfare.

On other occasions the definitions of social work are too narrow: they exclude from the category of social worker people who, it would fairly generally be agreed, come within its boundaries. Thus, definitions which emphasize the method of social casework or social work on a small scale leave out the social group worker and the social worker engaged in helping communities. We cannot expect very satisfying returns from the definitions already available, and this chapter will not attempt to add to their number.

This chapter will instead adopt an historical approach and attempt to introduce the subject of social work, firstly by detailed illustrations, and secondly by raising some general questions concerning the history of social work. We shall begin with an illustration of contemporary activity which everyone would agree was social work, and then contrast this with an example from the same social work agency but from a slightly earlier period. These two examples will illustrate themes which will be taken up in more detail later in the book. They are offered as good examples of the social work of their time, not as examples of good social work. This observation applies to all the illustrations in this book. Failure to observe this distinction between description and a positive evaluation has been responsible for some of the definition difficulties encountered in the social work literature. We have not seen clearly enough that 'social work' can refer both to an attempt and to a successful accomplishment.

The method of case study, whereby a detailed record of a particular situation is discussed in some depth, plays an important part in education for social work. This is so whether students are considering a situation confronting an individual or family, a larger group, or a neighbourhood or area. In the first case study in the present chapter we are able to see how the process of helping an individual or family (social casework) is experienced by the recipient of help. Such systematic emphasis on the perceptions of the consumer of social service is somewhat new in social work. It represents a perspective that is likely to bring considerable benefit to both the theory and the practice of social work.

Mary[2]

Mary is nineteen years of age, unmarried with a daughter of six months. She comes from a fairly prosperous middle-class family. Her father owns a successful antique business and her stepmother runs a secretarial agency. Mary's account of her experience with a social work agency refers back to the time before the baby was born. The account is given in her own words:

I knew that the news about the baby was not going to go down well at home. Mother was all right, but all father could think of was what the neighbours would say. At the time the business was not going well, and he had my sister to support at boarding school, so he said he could not afford to keep me and the baby. I used to get very upset. We had such rows. Every time I saw him we used to row, and I got to the stage that I simply would not stay in the house if I knew he was there. Mother was good, as I say, even though she was my stepmother, but in a sense she had to choose between us. I would try talking to my older brother, but he just said that I had to learn to cope. In fact he made me feel I had let everyone down, and that everyone was looking down at me for what I had done.

I went to the hospital, of course, as time went on. The doctor was rather abrupt – did I want the baby or didn't I? He thought I should go and see the medical social worker, but I found I could not talk to her. I went to her office once to get some forms and she kept asking me whether I wanted to see her again. I just said 'No'. I thought she was trying to take pity on me, and that if people knew I was going to see her they would know that I was not married.

4

Gradually I made up my mind that I wanted to keep the baby. Mother was not at all sure about this: she wanted to be convinced that I had really considered fully all the implications. A friend of hers suggested that it might help me if I went to see a family social worker. I agreed to go, but I was not sure that they would be able to help me. I expected that they would ask me a lot of questions, and find out a great deal about me – the kind of home that I came from, what my parents were like and so on. The main thing that worried me, though, was the fear I had that they would take the baby from me after it had been born. I thought that they would think that unmarried girls should not have babies and should not be allowed to keep them if they did. At the time I was getting a lot of help from my friend who was in the same predicament as myself. I used to get a lot of relief from unloading all my feelings, but mother thought it would be better if I went to see a social worker. She said that my friend was only my age and that the social worker would know more and understand more, and would be able to help, whereas my friend could only sit and listen.

The social worker I met at the family social service was really very good. I used to enjoy going, and I went every week. She was very understanding and never made me feel that I was completely to blame for the baby. She seemed to take me as I was and not look down on me. We used to talk over my plans, and she quite often made me think about things – important things. She was very comforting, particularly at the time when the baby's father decided that he would not marry me. She helped me to sort out going to hospital or to a mother and baby Home. I was not keen on the Home, because I had very odd ideas about who went there.

My relationship with the social worker was something of a strange relationship. At first I thought it was like the relationship between a pupil and a teacher, and that she only used to see me because she had to, and that if I did not go she would scold me. Once or twice I would miss going, but she never told me off. I began to wonder about that. When she did not tell me off for missing appointments I began to feel that she did not care whether I went there or not. I told her this, and she asked me what I was trying to prove. But I still wondered if she was seeing me just because it was her job, and not because she liked me in any way. I have decided that she does like me, because whenever I see her in the street she always stops and has a conversation.

I should think that it made a great difference seeing this social worker. I felt that her understanding wasn't false, that she wasn't just saying 'I understand' like a machine and just repeating it to everybody that came to see her. She really took an interest in my problem. It was funny the thing that made me stop going. It was after the baby was born, and everyone in the family was making such a fuss of her, and I hardly got a look in. Everybody wanted her. They wanted to pick her up and hold her. I took the baby along to see the social worker, and she behaved just like everyone else: she asked to hold her. I did resent that. It made me stop going. The social worker realized what I felt, and wrote to me saying that I must feel she had behaved as everyone else had. But it was no good.

It is clear that the case of Mary represents only one particular method of social work, that commonly known as social casework. The social worker could have decided, if the circumstances were appropriate, to help Mary through using groupwork: she could, for example, have asked Mary to join a group of girls in the same situation with the object of discussing their common problems and hence of reaching a more clear understanding of their difficulties. In other circumstances Mary might have been one of a number of girls all coming from the same area, though not necessarily sharing the same problem. In such a situation some kind of community-scale action might have seemed appropriate, perhaps in conjunction with social casework for certain individuals.

The record of Mary's reactions to casework help illustrates a number of aspects of the practice of social work whatever method is actually used. It shows the kind of problem that is brought to a social work agency, the kind of knowledge a social worker needs, and the sort of relationship established between a social worker and his or her 'client'. (The word 'client', here introduced for the first time, is often used half-apologetically with the reminder that whilst it is not altogether satisfactory none better has so far been suggested. In some situations its use does appear somewhat strained: in probation, for example, where it has been argued that the 'client' has little 'real' choice about whether to avail himself of the services of the probation officer or of the terms on which the service is available. In many respects, however, it seems a useful term, largely perhaps because of its persuasive character. It represents an attempt to recognize some element of dignity and of potential power in the person who receives social work help.)

From Mary's own account it is clear that the problem she presented to the social work agency could not be described simply as a case of illegitimacy. The fact that she was expecting a baby affected a whole range of relationships – those between herself and her father, her mother and father, herself and her brother, and so on. It is also apparent that she is none too clear about what the agency will be able to do for her, nor about how she herself intends to proceed. The social worker thus has the task of understanding the ramifications of her problem and of appreciating its meaning. She has to try to make sense of the situation.

In order to understand the situation facing this particular client, the social worker can begin to use knowledge of various kinds. She knows, for example, that different theories have been put forward to account for unmarried motherhood in general. Such theories fall into two main groups depending on whether the emphasis is given to psychological or to sociological factors. Thus, some writers on the subject would suggest that the illegitimate birth must be seen as the result of disturbed relationships within the girl's own family, whilst others would wish to examine the extent to which different social classes place different values on such

7

behaviour as pre-marital sex relations. The extent to which a social worker can rely on any of these approaches will be considered in a later chapter; at this point it is sufficient to note that, in looking at the problem Mary presents, the social worker has certain guidelines of a very general kind which will help in the attempt to understand the situation.

In the case of Mary we can also see the importance of the social worker's knowledge of the other social services that are available and could be appropriately used (the hospital or the mother and baby Home). Such knowledge includes both acquaintance with the services and some idea about the ways in which people might approach them. For example, it would be important in the situation facing Mary to realize that her feelings of shame, and perhaps of guilt, make it difficult for her to go to some of the agencies from which she might need help. Her own story indicates that precisely these feelings prevented her from making use of the services of the medical social worker. 'Asking for help' may seem to be such a simple and everyday occurrence, such obvious and justified behaviour, that we can easily overlook the difficulty it creates. It is part of the social worker's job to understand the particular difficulties of each client, whether the client is an individual or a group.

Finally, we can see from Mary's own account some of the significance of the relationship with the social worker. She did not find it easy to describe what the social worker did. For her, as for very many people, there appeared to be something very elusive about the activity. It resembled other familiar activities: it was like talking to friends, though the social worker did not take sides and Mary was not always sure that the social worker cared for her personally. Clearly, Mary valued her contact with the social worker, and also found the relationship somewhat complex. She seems to have valued the lack of censure and a predominant feeling that she was accepted, but she also behaved in ways that tested out her impression that the lack of censure on the part of the worker meant that she was simply indifferent to her situation.

Mrs Smith[3]

This is the case of a widow who was referred to the same
social work agency as Mary, but forty years earlier. The
ways in which she was helped and the case history recorded
help us to see some of the main changes that have occurred
in social work in the present century. (The term 'case' is
used very often in social work, and its use has been criticized
on the grounds that it 'turns people into dehumanized instances of something or someone's property'. The term,
however, refers to situations rather than to people, and its
main objective is to individualize rather than to generalize.
In this respect social work usage of the term differs significantly from the medical. In medicine 'case' is used to
identify a particular instance of a general category – this is
a case of chickenpox – so that certain general treatment
measures can be applied. In social work 'case' is intended to
particularize both the understanding of a situation and its
subsequent treatment.) Mrs Smith was referred to the
agency in November 1928. Her husband had died a month
before, and she was left with four daughters (aged 19, 18, 16
and 5) and three sons (10, 8 and 7). She required financial
help until her widow's pension was granted.

The social worker called on 20 November 1928 and the
following is her report in her own words:

I called to see Mrs Smith, combining our usual home
visit and the actual application for help. Mrs Smith looked
very clean and tidy, and was wearing a clean white
blouse and overall. She was dreadfully depressed and
worried. She said she had nothing but ill luck since moving into her present house. She was worried that she
might have to give it up unless the girls helped more by
turning over more of their money. She thinks it will be
some weeks before her pension comes through, and if we
can help her she is prepared to pay us back when it does
arrive. Her kitchen was spotlessly clean and tidy, though
rather bare, containing only a table, a couple of chairs,
and some pictures on the wall. There was a nice hearth

9

rug on the rather bare floor; the fireplace and the fender looked very bright and clean. Altogether I should say that mother and home made a very good impression. I saw the rent book. Rent was regularly paid and up to date. She gave me the names of people who would act as referees for her. She seemed straightforward and a reliable witness.

21 November I wrote to another branch asking for the referees to be seen. I wanted them to hear what opinions they held of Mrs Smith. Did her landlord find her a quiet, reliable tenant? Did she pay her rent regularly? Can she be recommended to my committee for help? I also wanted enquiry made from the employer of Mr Smith. I wanted to know if he knew anything about the man's family, what his opinion was of the man, and whether there was any trust or benefit fund from which his widow might get some help.

23 November The following replies were received: 'We have seen two of the referees, the landlord and a former neighbour. The landlord said that Mrs Smith at one time owed a great deal of rent, but she had cleared it in order to get into her new house. He could not say anything about her character, but thought that Mr Smith had been a decent fellow. We have also seen the former neighbour who said she had known the applicant for a number of years. She always found her quite steady and respectable.'

23 November Decision taken to help Mrs Smith financially. Such help to be repaid from the back-dated pension when it came through. The case was closed after mother had received the money and repaid it.

7 December 1929 A re-application was made when the Youth Employment Bureau sent the oldest daughter, Lilian, for a residential domestic job. Lilian called at the office. She said that she wanted to find a situation and would prefer to live in. She was tidily dressed in black, looked very small and was not particularly attractive. She said her mother was not unkind to her, but she was always nagging. She left her last employment because she could not get there by eight in the morning. She had to sweep the kitchen and light the stove after breakfast. She was not given any money for fares, and her work was a fifty-minute walk.

The same day a worker from the agency called at Lilian's former place of work, but the foreman would say nothing. Later the same day the employer telephoned to say that Lilian was not clean in her personal habits, and her fellow workers suspected her of theft. He said that she had once stayed out all night and refused to tell her mother where she had been. As a result of this information the agency decided that 'the girl should be urged to go into a Training Home'. (Training Homes were a kind of unofficial approved school for girls thought to be in some sort of moral danger.)

The agency confirmed with the Youth Employment Bureau that a Training Home would be suitable for Lilian, and the girl herself was seen. She said she was prepared to go. On 18 December the social worker called on Mrs Smith who was surprised to see her and even more astonished to hear that Lilian had been sent to the agency. She said that she could not spare Lilian, as she was now earning 14/- a week. She was convinced that the girl would not leave home, but she would tell Lilian that the social worker had called and she would persuade her to go along to the agency next week to complete the arrangements. Lilian did not appear. The case was closed.

In these extracts from the Smith case records, social work seems to consist of a series of relatively brief interventions in problem situations which are understood in a restricted way. In the first interview, for example, the problem is seen in the narrow terms of immediate financial shortage: no questions seem to have been raised in the social worker's mind concerning the possible reasons for the bareness of the home. On each occasion on which help was sought some judgments appear to have been crucial. Sometimes these are judgments made by the social worker – in the first interview, for instance, judgments about cleanliness and tidiness of both people and places occupy a significant position. At other times the judgments of those who are considered well-informed about the client are accepted – in the case of Lilian the former employer's impressions seem quite decisive.

There are several ways in which the case of Mary and that of Mrs Smith stand in marked contrast to each other. The social worker dealing with Mary seems to have been far less critical, far more concerned with the psychological dimensions of her relationship with Mary, and working on the basis of comparatively long-term treatment. These contrasts could be developed at length and the reader will no doubt have observed others of equal importance. At this stage in the argument, however, I wish to continue by using the two illustrations to begin to consider some of the problems of compiling a history of social work.

TOWARDS A HISTORY OF SOCIAL WORK

There are two difficulties that can be immediately illustrated from these two records. First, it is extremely difficult to obtain detailed records of the activities of social workers even in the comparatively recent past. We can obtain some idea of their probable activities from considering their theoretical writings, but those who write about social work are rarely describing their own practice, and we know from our own present experience that theoretical writing, even though it is not of a very high order, can systematically distort the picture of what actually occurs in social work practice. The second difficulty facing those who want to trace the historical development of social work concerns the ease with which we adopt attitudes of condemnation or praise towards past activities or ideas. (We have all probably reacted quite negatively whilst reading the second case record.) This tendency has been marked in many attempts to reconstruct the origins of modern social work in the second half of the nineteenth century. At times developments in the major social work organization of the period, the Charity Organization Society, have been used merely to provide a quarry for cautionary tales for progressive Fabians. The C.O.S. has attracted more blame than understanding and its founders have been treated as failures to the extent to which they failed to anticipate the twentieth century. In the attempt to write the history of social work, history has been turned into a kind of contemporary politics.

The failure to set the ideas of a particular period within the context of their time does not apply only to attempts to understand the immediate past of social work. It is often assumed that contemporary social work has a direct connection with earlier and well-established traditions of help. Smalley, for example, in a recent general text on social work states that 'The roots of social work are in man's earliest concern for his fellow man and for his group, his society. . . . Social workers still identify themselves with the long tradition of concern for human need and social stress'.[4] Klein has stated that social work 'represents a general social custom or habit of action of impressive and historical continuity'.[5] Such statements are not uncommon in the literature of social work, but they immediately raise two historical questions that have so far not been answered – largely because they have not been formulated with sufficient care. What is this tradition, and how is social work articulated with it? These are very large questions, and in this introductory work all that will be attempted is an illustration of the kinds of issues involved. We shall first look at an example of an attempt to trace the history of social work in the nineteenth century, and then turn our attention to the broader questions of the longer 'tradition' of helping from which social work is said to emanate: is it a single, unified tradition or are there a number of distinct views?

Accounts of the development of social work in the nineteenth century commonly single out as a decisive influence the work and thought of Thomas Chalmers. Chalmers, 'a mathematician by training, an economist from interest, a Church scholar by calling',[6] is known in the history of social work largely because of the way in which he organized help to the poor outside the sphere of the official Poor Law. Between 1819 and 1823 he was in charge of the Glasgow parish of St John's, where he established a parochial form of care which relied very heavily on encouraging self-help, restraint in the giving of alms, and the careful investigation of the individual case. 'It is not enough that you give money, you must give it with judgment. You must give your time and attention. You must descend to the trouble of examination: for instance, will charity corrupt him into slothfulness? What is his particular necessity?'[7] The system Chalmers devised combined ideas fairly common at the time with a rigorous and systematic organization. Some of his ideas resemble those espoused by the famous Charity Organization Society later in the century, but more is often claimed for them than family resemblance. The work of Chalmers is seen as a direct causal influence on the ideas and organization of later philanthropic ventures.

This seems plausible, but the point to be made in the present argument about the compilation of the history of social work is that no evidence has been produced to show the ways in which the work of Chalmers exerted influence on those seeking to remodel charitable work in the last quarter of the nineteenth century. There is in fact some evidence which suggests that the work of Chalmers was rediscovered after the main lines of reorganization had already been laid down. It was then adopted as a gloss on what was then the contemporary reality rather than received as an original inspiration. C. S. Loch, for many years the general secretary of the Society, was of the opinion that 'when the C.O.S. was established in London . . . I should doubt if the fundamental conceptions of Dr Chalmers were then appreciated'.[8]

It is also worth noting that Masterman's selection of the writings of Chalmers published in 1900 suggests that the published works of Chalmers had been out of circulation for some time prior to the foundation of the Charity Organization Society. 'The name of Chalmers is familiar to many. . . . But his writings are very little known even to the most studious and active workers in the social field. In the first place, they are not easily accessible. They have been out of print for nearly half a century.'[9]

Further discussion of this particular question would be inappropriate in the present work. It has been raised simply to illustrate that the history of social work even in the last 100 years is not as clear as it is often assumed to be.

The example of the presumed influence of Thomas Chalmers illustrates how far we are from a satisfactory account even of the recent past of social work. The position is even more unsatisfactory when we widen the canvas and seek to understand the extent to which social work is connected with much older traditions. Again we can only illustrate the kind of issue involved by raising two questions: what, if anything, is lacking in the fairly commonly expressed view, that the modern social worker treads in the steps of St Francis of Assisi; is there something distinctively Christian in the 'origin' of social work?

Writers who stress that the roots of modern social work are to be found in Christian ideas and practice overlook the immediate and the more remote past. In the immediate past they neglect the extent to which modern social work is a substitute for religion. As Huntington observed in 1892: 'The "service of humanity" is set forward as a substitute for adherence to creeds and dogmas and formularies of devotion, or the development of ethical systems.'[10] More distantly it is possible to discern in Christian tradition itself a number of different attitudes to 'helping the poor and unfortunate', one of which, at any rate, is not readily reconcilable with modern social work. It used to be assumed that as far as the practice of 'charitable' work was concerned, Christian theory and practice in the Middle Ages could teach no lessons to the modern practitioner. The Charity Organization Society and the Webbs were on opposite sides on many questions of social policy, but they both agreed that the mediaeval church took a fundamentally wrong position, when in its teaching on alms-giving and the works of mercy, it emphasized the benefits that would accrue to the alms-giver and advocated indiscriminate help to all who appeared to be in need. This emphasis on response to need without any investigation of the circumstances undoubtedly represents one strand in the traditional Christian teaching on charity. Equally clearly it seems to be incompatible with two assumptions made by the nineteenth-century social worker which form an important part of the basis of modern social work. The practice of indiscriminate help for the good of the donor's spiritual health runs counter to the idea that the kind of help appropriate can only be determined after investigation and some kind of appraisal of the particular situation, and coupled with this the belief that helping people is such a complex activity that the uninitiated may well do more harm than good.

In so far, then, as Christian tradition is represented by the views we have been examining, it is not easy to see how it is compatible with some aspects at least of contemporary social work. But Christian tradition is more complex than this: we cannot accept the simple account of mediaeval thought presented by the Webbs or by C. S. Loch. Tierney has recently shown how frequently the problem of indiscriminate charity was discussed by the canonists. Gratian perhaps represents a typical position when he advocates both openhanded liberality and cautious discrimination. The bishops were to be generous to the poor, but 'in this generosity due measure is to be applied both of things and of persons; of things, that not everything is to be bestowed on one but on various individuals . . . of persons, that we give first to the just, then to sinners, to whom, nevertheless, we are forbidden to give not as men but as sinners'.[11] A more close insistence on the virtues of careful investigation is to be found in the work of another canonist, the *Summa* of Rufinus:

> It should be known that we ought not to show ourselves generous indiscriminately to all who come. But it should be known that in providing hospitality these four things

are to be considered: the quality of the one seeking alms, the resources of the giver, the cause of the request, and the amount requested. The quality of the one asking – whether he is honest or dishonest; the resources of the one giving – whether they can suffice for all or only for some; the cause of the request – whether a man asks only for food for the love of God or says he is sent as a preacher and therefore claims due stipend from you; the amount requested – whether it is excessive or reasonable. If the one who asks is dishonest, and especially if he is able to seek his food by his own labour and neglects to do so, so that he chooses rather to beg or steal, without doubt nothing is to be given to him, but he is to be corrected . . . unless perchance he is close to perishing from want, for then, if we have anything we ought to give indifferently to all such.[12]

In this quotation we can see the care with which various criteria are laid down to guide the decisions of those called upon to help other people. This kind of categorized prudence seems to have little in common with the approach, say, of St Francis of Assisi, but both approaches are emphatically within the Christian tradition.

When we begin to search for the tradition in which social work is thought to be rooted are we correct in looking exclusively to Christian sources? This is a very difficult question to answer, but historical research into the differing traditions that constituted the ancient world suggests some lines of thought that could be profitably followed.

Bolkestein,[13] in an important study of charity and poor relief in pre-Christian times, found both similarities and differences between the different societies of the ancient world. Thus, in all the societies he examined he found that some groups of people were always the object of special moral duties, namely parents, old people and friends. He assumed that the special consideration shown to such groups is common to all societies at a certain level of cultural development. However, he also noted important differences. The Egyptians and the Israelites stressed their obligations towards strangers who were in need or poor strangers, whereas the Greeks felt under an obligation to those placed at a disadvantage by being in strange surroundings. In the Mosaic Law hospitality was a kind of poor relief, but in Greece it was mainly a relationship between nobles or merchants. The Romans had an even narrower concept of hospitality: it was obligatory only in the case of foreigners of the same standing as the host, and was seen as a means of obtaining good relations with them.

If we consider the place of the poor in the ancient religious systems we again find a strong contrast between the ideas of the Eastern and the Western world. The Egyptians from the earliest times believed that God was the benefactor of mankind, and their later ideas envisaged that he was especially the protector of the poor against the rich and the powerful. The Israelites also believed this, but no trace of beliefs of this kind can, according to Bolkestein, be found in Greece or in Rome. In these societies the rich were seen as the favourites of the gods because they were in a position to make the largest sacrifices.

Whether we are concerned with the moral, the religious or the political systems of the ancient world we find that the Egyptians and the Israelites gave the poor a special position denied them by the Greeks and the Romans. Why this should be so is clearly an important and interesting question, but enough has been said to indicate the necessity of treating with some scepticism the frequent assertion that the roots of social work are to be found in 'Graeco-Roman-Christian' traditions. Such assertions should be questioned in three main ways. First, the assumption of unity in the source of social work seems unsubstantiated. Second, we must again face the largely unexplored question of the paths along which ancient traditions reached the more modern social worker. Third, we should be careful not to treat as identical ideas and organizational forms which appear at different points in history in apparently similar form. Thus, the form and practice of charity amongst the early Christians seem to resemble closely the combinations of compassion and material help found in the ancient societies of the East. Yet this must not lead us to overlook that the conceptual basis was different. For the Christian benevolence to the poor was part of the love one should have for the neighbour and both were part of the love of God. In Egyptian morality charity was not founded on love.

SUMMARY

In this chapter we have tried to show contemporary social work activity through the eyes of a particular recipient. The case of Mary shows at least some of the attitudes a social worker would adopt, whatever method of work he or she was using, and some of the ways in which he or she would attempt to be helpful. This case was contrasted with an earlier instance from the same social work agency which could be taken as reasonably typical of much of the social work on an individual basis of the preceding fifty years or so. The example of Mrs Smith showed a somewhat different activity, though again most people at the time would have called it social work.

The contrast led us to consider much wider questions concerning the history of social work. These questions are of academic interest: it is clearly important in any educational subject to trace developments over time. In looking at the history of social work – as far as it can be said to have one – we can establish two important conclusions. First, commonly accepted views which summarize the history of social work can be taken only as indicating a range of unanswered questions. Second, social work is very much a product of our time, and we will find at best only parallels with other times and other societies. Modern social work can only be understood within the context of modern society: we can ask useful questions about the ways in which 'social problems' were defined in mediaeval times or in the ancient world, but we cannot assume that we are thereby enquiring into the roots of modern social work. In an important sense there is no mediaeval or ancient social work.

Questions about the 'origins' of modern social work raise genuinely historical questions, but they are also important for the person considering the possibility of social work as a career. Such a person is often trying to discover how far social work can be seen as connected in some special way with Christianity or with some other general way of looking at and behaving towards the world.

NOTES

[1] Devine, E., *The Spirit of Social Work*, New York, 1911.

[2] The case of Mary (suitably disguised), is taken from the sample of sixty-one cases interviewed in the research project conducted by John Mayer and Noel Timms into the reactions of former clients of the Family Welfare Association, London. See 'Clash in Perspective between Social Worker and Client' *Social Casework*, January 1969.

[3] The case of Mrs Smith is taken from a sample of cases from the Family Welfare Association selected in connection with the author's study of historical developments of social work practice. See 'Social Work in Action – A Historical Study', *Case Conference*, Part I, April 1961, Part II, May 1961.

[4] Smalley, R., *The Practice of Social Work*, New York: Columbia University Press, 1967, pp. vii/viii.

[5] Klein, P., 'The Social Theory of Professional Social Work', *Contemporary Social Theory*, ed. H. E. Barnes et al., Appleton-Century, 1940, p. 754.

[6] Young, P., and Ashton, E., *British Social Work in the Nineteenth Century*, London: Routledge & Kegan Paul, 1956, p. 69.

[7] Chalmers, T., *On Charity*, ed. Marsterman, N., London: Constable, 1900, p. 221.

[8] Loch, C. S., 'Doctor Chalmers and Charity Organisation', *Charity Organisation Review*, August 1897.

[9] Chalmers, T., op. cit.

[10] Huntington, J., 'Philanthropy and Morality', *International Journal of Ethics*, October 1892. See also the argument in Scheler, M., *The Nature of Sympathy* (Routledge & Kegan Paul, 1954) that 'the modern idea of benevolence (humanitarianism, philanthropy, etc.) has been "worked up" entirely from motives of resentment against patriotism and the Christian love of God and the person', pp. 99-100.

[11] Tierney, B., *Medieval Poor Law*, Berkeley, University of California Press, 1959, pp. 55-6.

[12] Tierney, B., op. cit., p. 59.

[13] Bolkestein, H., *Wohltätigkeit und Armenpflege im Vorchristlichen Altertum* (Charity and Poor-Relief in Pre-Christian Times). My account of poor-relief in pre-christian times is based on that given by Bolkestein.

2

Social Work
in Organizations

CONTEMPORARY SOCIAL WORKERS are to be found within a variety of organizations. Probation officers work in the courts of law and in the prison after-care service; children's departments of the local authorities employ child-care officers; medical social workers (until quite recently known as almoners) are to be found in hospitals and in some local authority health departments; psychiatric social workers work in child guidance clinics, mental hospitals and the local authority health department. In addition social workers are employed by a range of voluntary or non-statutory organizations, for example, the Family Service Units, which give special help to 'problem families', or the various children's societies associated with the different religious denominations.

Each kind of organization plays an important part in the formation of the social work carried out under its auspices. This applies to any of the methods used by social workers. Thus, a report on the method of community work states that

> Statutory and voluntary organizations which employ community workers (or have members of their staff who devote part of their time to community work) do so as a means of carrying out the organization's purposes, for example, the promotion of voluntary services for the elderly, the development of a local mental health service, the strengthening of neighbourly relationships, or the expansion of facilities for the handicapped. The purpose

of the employing organization sets limits to the kind of community work and has a strong influence on the direction it will take.[1]

Modern social work began in the voluntary sector. It was based originally on the assumption that the State's role in welfare should be clearly and vigorously circumscribed. The statutory Poor Law existed as a last resort which would ensure that people at least did not die from penury, but help on any other terms should not be given in what was described as a 'wholesale' manner. Help to be effective had, on this argument, to be given in a retail way, and it was the voluntary bodies that claimed the right to investigate and decide on the individual case.

Gradually social workers began to operate from bases other than that provided by the voluntary family welfare organization. The first extension into the hospital field in 1894 was still within the voluntary sector, but the recognition of probation officers in the Probation of Offenders Act of 1907 marks the appearance of the first 'official' social worker. In the 1930s psychiatric social work started in the voluntary and experimental child guidance clinics, as well as in certain hospitals. After the Second World War, psychiatric social workers began to move into the local authority as mental health workers. The last major organizational expansion came with the Children's Act in 1948. This created a new department in the local authority specially concerned with the needs of the child deprived of normal home life.

This presents with extreme brevity an outline of the points at which social workers became connected to different organizational settings. This development of social work is frequently described as uneven and we are often called upon to mourn what is represented as 'illogical' and 'piecemeal' progression. The fact that it is never made clear what it would be like for social work to have developed 'logically' or 'evenly' is yet another example of the failure previously noted to grasp what it means to understand something historically. The purpose of the present chapter, however, is not the presentation of a detailed chronology of the way in which social work has developed in each service, important though that is. Rather this chapter will attempt to describe some of the main aspects of social work in each service and, finally, to raise some questions of a general nature. In describing social work in each of its main 'settings' we shall try to emphasize aspects that relate to essential functions. This is because the actual specialist names by which workers in the different fields are known may be used less and less in the future, especially when a single professional association of social workers is formed. More importantly, the Seebohm Committee of Enquiry into the personal social services of the local authority has recently recommended the establishment of a general social service department which would undertake 'responsibilities extending well beyond the responsibilities of existing local authority departments' and would include:

(a) the present services provided by children's departments;
(b) the welfare services provided under the National Assistance Act 1948;
(c) education and child guidance welfare services;
(d) the home help service, mental health social work services, other social work services and day nurseries provided by local health departments;
(e) certain social welfare currently undertaken by some housing departments.[2]

If this proposal is accepted it will clearly lead to a considerable reorganization of social work in the local authority sphere, and many of the detailed regulations presently governing the practice of social work will have to be changed. Yet the main functions (e.g., of caring for deprived children, the mentally subnormal and so on) will be, if anything, more important than ever, and it is to these functions that most space will be devoted in the present chapter.

The child guidance clinic

Service for the emotionally disturbed child is available through the local authority (there were 359 clinics in 1966 treating a total of slightly more than 57,000 children) or through certain hospital boards (in 1963, for example, hospitals saw over 25,000 new patients and over 181,000 attendances were recorded). In addition a range of residential provision is available for the 'maladjusted child'. This form of provision has grown steadily with the development of special educational provision for handicapped persons of all kinds. Between 1953 and 1962 the number of maladjusted boys in maintained and non-maintained schools increased from 705 to something over 1,600 and of maladjusted girls from 170 to 380. In January 1961 a total of 1,700 children who were maladjusted were in independent boarding schools.

The psychiatric social worker in child guidance fulfils two important functions: she helps in the formation of a diagnosis of the problem facing the child and his parents, and she co-operates in the treatment of this problem. Child guidance clinics are usually staffed by a psychiatrist (a medically qualified person with experience and quite often training in psychiatric medicine), a psychologist (a person with university and often clinical training in the measurement of intelligence, personality traits, etc., and the treatment of learning difficulties) and a psychiatric social worker (a trained social worker who has specialized in the field of mental disturbance). The combination of the knowledge and skill of these three disciplines represents the special diagnosis and treatment available in the child guidance clinic. Hence the considerable emphasis given to the idea of team work.

This is not an idea, however, that should be uncritically accepted as a description of what 'really happens'. In particular the role of the psychiatric social worker in 'the team' is and has always been somewhat ambiguous. Psychiatric medicine clearly has a special contribution to make to the

24

diagnosis and treatment of the disturbed child, and so has the psychologist, but the psychiatric social worker seems to be in the position of the 'marginal man'. What can he (or she) contribute to a diagnosis that a good psychiatrist would not observe, and what special features mark her treatment of the mother or father as distinct? These questions have not often been squarely faced, though they are answerable. As social work gains more confidence in the study of groups wider than the family (e.g., neighbourhood groups of various kinds), and as the study of the family escapes from the notions that families are or should be fashioned after the same model, we can expect to see a more convincing demonstration of the special area of knowledge on which the social worker can rely for his opinion on the causation of a particular problem. This in turn will have implications for the direction of his or her treatment efforts.

Already the psychiatric social worker is in a good position from which to exploit this wider knowledge, since he is usually in close touch with the parents of the children concerned. The following extract from a first treatment interview illustrates some of the problems arising from this contact:

> *Jean* is eight years old, the middle child of a family consisting of mother (a nurse), father (a social worker), Dawn, 14 and Roger, 6. Jean was referred to the clinic by her mother for four main problems: poor school work, jealousy of Roger – she had pinched and bitten him, and mother had pinched and bitten her – her dislike of her father, and stealing from the home.

It was decided to take Jean on for treatment, which meant that she would be seen weekly by the psychiatrist, while her mother had an interview with the psychiatric social worker. The psychiatrist explained what would happen, and that his interviews with Jean would be confidential. After some preliminary discussion the psychiatric social worker took Jean's mother to her room. As mother left she touched Jean, as if to give her reassurance.

In the social worker's room Jean's mother said that she

thought that Jean felt upset. The social worker suggested that perhaps mother herself felt upset. She agreed. She had not quite expected the psychiatrist to talk over the problems so openly with Jean. She went on to talk of Jean having in her possession a fountain pen belonging to a school friend. Mother had threatened to tell the head teacher when it seemed that Jean was not going to return it, and Jean cried so bitterly that it made mother feel she had been very cruel. The social worker said that perhaps mother felt she had been rather cruel to bring Jean to the clinic, and that it might be like bringing her to the headmaster. Mother said she was not sure about that. There was quite a long pause. The social worker then suggested that mother might well be wondering what she had let herself in for by coming to the clinic. Mother agreed that this was so. She felt that she ought to have managed on her own, and she just felt 'silly' coming. The social worker asked if she could explain a little more what she meant by 'silly'.

Mother appeared not to notice this question, and went on to talk about her husband's work which was connected with people going into mental hospital. She was very worried about the effect of this work on her own nerves. Her husband did not talk a great deal about this work, but what he did tell her made her worry. She knew that she was being 'silly'. The social worker suggested to Jean's mother that she seemed to be concerned about what coming to the clinic meant. Perhaps it was associated with people who were thought to be mentally ill in some way, and possibly the mother was worrying about Jean in this connection. Quite often parents did feel somewhat afraid of the clinic, and thought that simply because they took their child there it must mean he or she was somehow mentally ill.

The social worker is here seen fulfilling what can be described as a very important boundary function. The social worker is, as it were, standing at the entrance to the service and attempting to recognize the feelings of those who come wanting to use what the service has to offer. To fulfil this function in the child guidance clinic the social worker has to feel securely part of the service which she has to interpret to the client, and has to be aware of the range of possible significance the particular service can take on for different people. The clinic can be seen, for instance, as the place where bad children are taken for some kind of control or punishment or where bad, ineffective parents are themselves punished for their failure to rear their children successfully. At other times the clinic is significantly associated in the mind of the client with ideas of the detection and cure of madness.

The psychiatric social worker in the local health authority

Increasing attention is being paid to treating the mentally ill and other groups of disadvantaged people, as far as possible, within the community. A movement away from exclusive reliance on institutional care was evident during and after the Second World War, but it received considerable impetus under the Mental Health Act, 1959. At 31 December 1967, more than 87,000 mentally ill or psychopathic patients and almost 97,500 subnormal or severely retarded patients were the responsibility of local health authorities. The movement to which reference has been made is often described as the 'community care' movement. This is a fairly vague phrase, but one aspect clearly refers to the desire to deal with mental illness in ways that depart from the nineteenth-century policy of removing mentally sick people from 'normal' community life and keeping them for very long periods in hospitals in isolated parts of the country. Programmes of community care can be based on the mental hospital or the local authority. In order to illustrate the kinds of task such a programme may involve we shall examine briefly not detail from one individual case, but extracts from the diary of a local authority mental welfare officer covering just one day. (The bare essential details were later amplified in discussion):

9.15. Called to see Mr and Mrs R. They have a severely subnormal son, and have requested help. Discussed the possibility of attendance at the Day Centre to be opened later this year. Mrs R. seemed reluctant. She seems to be worried about what will happen to him when he is away from her. Mr R. said very little. What he did say suggested that he was still feeling very guilty about his son, possibly blaming himself because there is some vague recollection of mental illness on his side of the family.

10 a.m. Home Visit to Miss L. (60) caring for her sister (57) recently discharged from mental hospital. The sister was in bed, sitting up reading, and behaving in a generally demanding way. She called to Miss L. three times whilst I was present, asking for the newspaper, drinks etc. Miss L. seemed very tired, but she did not complain. I talked with her about her previous life with her sister who had always been the clever and pretty one of the family; everyone had always taken second place to her. She had in fact achieved a successful career in music, but now she had no interest in it at all. I suggested that Miss L. should go and see her doctor, since she was looking so exhausted. I arranged to contact him, since Miss L. is always somewhat diffident, and I said I would put her in touch with the local branch of the W.V.S. who ran a sitter-in service. This would enable her to get to the doctor at least. The sister, whom I saw also, still seems very depressed. I can see little signs of being able to help Miss L. to break the strong pattern of subservience to her sister, but I hope that by encouraging her to look after her health and by supplying occasional relief, in the form of sitters, etc., I can help her to maintain the present pattern.

11.15 Returned to the office. Telephoned the G.P. re Miss L. The doctor wanted to meet me at the home of Mr G. Mrs G. had called him to see her husband who was acting very strangely: he had not been at work for a week, spent most of the day pacing up and down the garden talking to imaginary people. On two occasions he had been violent with her in the night. The doctor thought it sounded as if admission to a mental hospital would be required and he would be glad of my opinion. I met the doctor at the house. He talked to Mrs G. and then went into the garden to see Mr G. I obtained details of Mr G.'s behaviour and then went to join Mr G. and the doctor who had by this time returned to the house. Mr G. seemed very wild and distraught. The doctor said he should go to hospital. I telephoned for the ambulance. Helped Mrs G. to get Mr G. ready. I had to spend quite a lot of time explaining to her what would happen and outline to Mr G. what would occur within the next few hours. He was at first very resistant to the idea of going into a mental hospital, but as I talked quietly with him he calmed down. The fact that his wife would be coming in the ambulance with him seemed to reassure him. Getting Mr G. to hospital took about four hours, and it was 5 p.m. by the time I returned to the office.

8 p.m. I attended a meeting of a local residents' association. It had been called to consider what action should be taken to protest about the proposal of the local authority to build a hostel for the mentally ill in the locality. This was an informal meeting. I outlined new developments in the care of the mentally ill and tried to show why care in the community entailed at least partly care by the community. I also encouraged them to talk about the kind of patient they thought might come to the hostel. Many residents seemed particularly worried about their children; others were afraid that the value of their houses would decline. It was agreed at the end of the meeting that further discussion would be helpful.

In this summary of a working day we can see the social worker once again concerned with helping people to make use of the social services that exist, and exploring the kinds of feelings that sometimes prevent them from doing so. In addition the local authority social worker is also involved in the admission of patients to hospital, sometimes when compulsory powers have to be used. The service which he represents has, like many others, an important dual function – both of providing care for the mentally subnormal and the mentally ill, and also of seeing that people who participate, directly or indirectly, in that care do not themselves suffer unduly. This very difficult set of tasks was carried out by the social worker whose day of work we have been following in the case of Miss L., and of the residents' meeting that she attended.

Psychiatric social work in the mental hospital

The following illustration from the work of a psychiatric social worker in a mental hospital shows the worker participating fully in treatment. It should be noted that the treatment being carried out is one using the method of groupwork rather than casework, which as we have seen concentrates much more on the individual. The extract could be used to illustrate a number of important points – for example, the economical use of interpretation – but in the present context it indicates some of the problems involved in trying to help people who are, in varying degrees, mentally ill. In particular the conductor of the group has to cope with the problem of being one of the group and also someone who is trying to help. This means becoming quite deeply involved in the feelings present in the group, and at times these can be strong and distressing. Thus, one of the members calls attention to the way in which the group conductor expresses her view of what the group is feeling: she always refers to the depression, the isolation, and so on which *we*, the group members, are feeling. Does she really include herself? The conductor says that she does, but this then seems to mean, for one member at least, that the conductor cannot help at all. To which the conductor replies: 'You make it sound as if the only help in the group comes from me and I must be preserved on a pedestal without human problems. Then when I tell you that I have human feelings I become one of the helpless ones like you with no power to help you or myself.' This seems to represent a complex of problems facing all social workers, irrespective of the field in which they work: how far identification with and differentiation from clients is possible and desirable, and the elusive nature of social work expertise.

RECORD OF PART OF A GROUP MEETING

This record is part of one of the weekly meetings of a group which had been meeting with the same membership for eighteen months. The members were originally referred to the psychiatric out-patient department of a hospital and were thought to be isolated people whose symptoms were the result of failure to relate to others.

The Group:
Joan: a single woman of 40 with a long history of depression and panic attacks when travelling. Works as a secretary for a large firm. Is at present living in hospital but coming up daily to work and weekly to the group.

Jim: a single man of 36 once diagnosed as schizophrenic. Has difficulty in getting on with men in authority and never keeps his girl friends. Has just completed a retraining course as a fitter and started a new job in a factory.

George: a single man of 37 living with his mother. Acts the clown but is despairing of the future and often talks of suicide. Has no friends.

Mary: a single woman of 38 who has not worked for 10 years and who lives with her father. She gets severely depressed and has recently been discharged from the same hospital that Joan is in.

Vera: a single woman of 41, very successful in business but who feels persecuted by the world and especially by her brothers.

Stephen: a single man of 35, successful in a professional job but very isolated socially.

Group conductor: a single woman of 36, a P.S.W. with some groupwork training.

Group meeting:

Vera: You said at the end last time, Stephen, that you saw things differently from before and it was a matter of welcoming things – what did you mean?

Stephen: Well, it's hard to explain – but I try to make myself welcome things – be open to them and let them come in – not shut them all out.

George: It's whether you rebel or submit, that's what I say. You haven't any choice, you're a rat in a trap. Take me for example. I know it's the end for me when the firm moves to Mortlake in January – I know I shan't survive and I'll just stay at home in bed. How do you welcome that?

Mary: George, you always talk as if you can only go to Mortlake or go to bed – but you could get another job, couldn't you, or maybe ask the personnel man if you can stay in Victoria?

George: I've told you it's no good. Nothing is any good and I might as well stay in bed and that'll be the end as I'll never get up again. I know that. What I want to know is why us? Why do we get stuck so that we're shifted around and have to rebel or submit? Haven't our firms any gratitude to us? Look at all the people who idle the day away and what do they get? A pay rise – and they don't spend their evenings in places like this. I tell you, they should be here having therapy, not us.

Conductor: We seem to be talking about the difficulties of taking responsibility for ourselves – it's so much easier to shift it on to other people.

Stephen: Things look different when you welcome them, and it's not just a mood like you said [to conductor]. I was annoyed when you said it was the differences between a depressed

32

mood and how we see life from that, and a non-depressed mood. It's much more than a mood it's a way of looking at life.

Vera: Well, when I get out of bed and it's foggy and I know the trains are late again and I'll have to stand – well, what do I do? Say welcome to the fog?

Stephen: Yes, in a way. I used to get depressed at the weekends and think all I had to come was another week of work and I tried to make myself welcome it. Even going down the street – you can see people and welcome them or you can shut them out – it's awful how people don't even look at each other.

Conductor: This happens in the group too – we won't even look at each other, let alone try to share feelings.

Jim: [who has come in late] I do this at work. It's a huge factory – like streets all full of people going to their own jobs and I walked by them with a haughty air saying 'keep off'. Now I'm getting to know some – a boy drilled through his finger today and I got to know him and he's quite a nice chap – ordinary not stuck up. Another one I need to keep in with because he does my heavy sawing. I was treating him like a machine and today he stuck up for me to the foreman and he's human too.

Mary: You don't want to have to ask a human for help, did you?

Jim: No, I expect you're right. I either want to be completely independent or completely looked after – not in between.

Vera: Will you stick the job, Jim?

Jim: I want to keep it for 6 months – it's good experience and I'm learning to work faster. I've never worked so hard in my life. It's piece rates – we all work hard. If I can feel

33

	better towards the men I work with I shall manage, I think.
George:	That's it – you're afraid of feelings being roused in you towards the men and getting out of control. It's fear, really.
Vera:	I have difficulty at work because men seem to resent me doing my job well. There's a man I sit next to and he's always getting at me, quite unnecessarily. This morning . . . [a long account of how this man had made what Vera felt to be a personal attack on her – she complained and he apologized].
George:	Well some people are like that – he should come to the group.
Conductor:	Perhaps we could look at why Vera is still upset by this episode which she seems to have handled quite successfully. Whether the man has difficulties isn't our problem, but Vera's angry hurt feelings are.
Stephen:	Well, men don't like women being tactless and knowing best.
Vera:	But what am I to do? I am good at my job – better than he is. What am I to do – be a doormat?
Stephen:	It happens here too. You and Jim used to fight – you attacked him with clever remarks and then thought he was personally cruel back to you and then you went off in a huff.
Vera:	I really don't know what to do. I do see what's happening – what am I to do – sit around like a doormat with 'welcome' written all over me.
Conductor:	Perhaps the difficulty is here – Vera's last remark was witty and clever and makes Stephen's idea of welcome look stupid. It seemed to arise from Vera feeling attacked. Perhaps there is a difference between using your brain and using it as a defensive weapon.

34

George: Women would be better off being women and leaving brains alone. They shouldn't be over men either.

Conductor: Perhaps that applies here too. It might be easier if the group were taken by a man – or you feel it might be. Women shouldn't have brains or power.

George: That's what you always do. You are just touchy. You take any remark about women in power as referring to yourself. It's nonsense. No one listens to you anyway.

Vera: Why do you always deny you mean P. when you say that kind of thing? We all know what you mean.

Conductor: Yes – you do all know what he means and since he says it there's no need for anyone else to say it. George has taken on for the group the job of making attacks on me, then denying them, and then being attacked by the group, not for the remark but for denying its meaning.

Stephen: I've kept a diary since I joined the group and I found that for the first few months I used to write down what you said and then all the reasons why you were wrong and why what you said was no help.

Mary: Is she still always wrong?

Stephen: No – she wasn't always wrong then – but it's hard to take help from a woman.

Joan: I've wanted to ask you for some time – you say here 'we are feeling depressed – or isolated – or something'. Do you mean you feel it too?

Conductor: Yes. I wouldn't mean to use 'we' unless I included myself.

Joan: Well then, how can you help if you have all the same problems as we have? [She starts to cry.] I can't see what we can do if you are as bad as us.

35

Conductor: You make it sound as if the only help in the group comes from me and I must be preserved on a pedestal without human problems. Then when I tell you I have human feelings I become one of the helpless ones like you with no power to help you or myself.

Jim: It is a very black and white way to see you. Either perfect or helpless. Perhaps the difference is that you don't come here to solve your problems but we do – the jobs we do here are different.

Conductor: But we all share the job of helping each other.

Stephen: But we make this so hard because we hide from each other. I hide behind reason and Vera behind her brains and George behind his clowning –

Conductor: And Joan behind her tears [Joan has been crying for some time].

Jim: Why do we hide?

Vera: It's fear, I think – fear of really meeting people. Perhaps we would get hurt if we let ourselves mind about people.

Stephen: It's a fear we got from our parents. If they didn't really love us and want us then what was wrong with us? We must have been monsters if our own parents didn't want us.

Joan: But I was a good child – I did everything I was told. I wasn't a monster.

Stephen: I'm not saying you were – all I'm saying is that as children we thought this and now we can't let people really meet us in case they find the monster.

Jim: That's right – I feel like a monster when I go glowering down the works stopping people from even saying 'good morning' to me. I even feel my face is like a monster's, and I am the monster I fear they'll find.

36

George: That's all eye-wash. You're afraid of getting too fond of other men and of what the world will say.

Jim: Well I am afraid of that, yes, but it's much more than that. I get afraid of the whole world.

Conductor: It sometimes seems, George, as if your fear of your love for men serves to hide other fears. I wonder if we could ask instead why don't you relate to women?

George: Well, I've told you – they leave me cold. [He turns to Jim]. You just avoid your problem by saying you feel a monster – you mean a homosexual. Isn't that so, Stephen?

Conductor: It seems that you are forming a homosexual club in the group – you answered my question about women by turning to Jim and including Stephen. It's a way of ignoring half the group – or a way of living that allows you to ignore the existence of half the world. Why?

Mary: What about your mother, George? You don't ignore her, do you?

George: No. You know I think the world of her and I'd be lonely – no, I'd be dead without her. But it's only a matter of time – she's 76.

THE CHILD CARE OFFICER

On 31 March 1967 over 69,000 children were in the care of local authorities: in 1966 28 per cent of the child care officers were professionally qualified, and nearly a half had been in the service under two years. The child care officer has a job which in some respects is inadequately described in her title. Very little of her (or his) time is given to the actual care of children, since day-to-day care is largely in the hands of residential staff, foster parents and natural parents. Her concern for the child, her responsibility to

37

ensure the best care possible, often entails direct work with people other than the child, so that much of her time is spent talking with foster parents and prospective foster parents, helping mothers and fathers to cope with the stress of family life so that they can retain the custody and the care of their children, supporting and learning from residential staff in an attempt to arrange the best form of substitute care where separation is inevitable. Yet the title at least accurately represents the concern of the Curtis Committee that led directly to the establishment of the new children's department in 1948, that some particular official should be held responsible for seeing that the interests of the child are safeguarded, that adequate plans are made for its future, and that someone stands by for as long as necessary to help it make sense of what is happening.

The work of the child care officer embraces a large range of tasks, adoption, foster home selection and supervision, work with residential care units, and giving families such help as may prevent their children from being received into the care of the children's department. This latter type of work, called very often 'preventive', was given a new emphasis by the Children and Young Persons Act of 1963 which gave local authorities the duty

> to make available such advice, guidance and assistance as may promote the welfare of children by diminishing the need to receive children into or keep them in care . . . or to bring children before a juvenile court; and any provisions made by a local authority under this sub-section may, if the local authority think fit, include provision for giving assistance in kind, or in exceptional circumstances in cash.

Limitation of space prevents each type of work being illustrated. Two areas of work have been chosen – work in connection with the reception of children into care, and work with foster parents.

Mr. and Mrs W.

Mr and Mrs W. and their four chilren, aged 4, 5, 7 and 8 were evicted by their private landlord after a long history of poor payment of rent. Mrs W. was attending a day hospital: she was extremely anxious, unable to be alone and always trying to prevent her husband going out – this had contributed to his very poor work record. Mr W. was also rather an anxious person, further handicapped by the loss of a leg in a motor accident when he was a child. Despite the unfavourable environment the children were free from emotional disturbance, and showed real warmth in their relationships with their parents.

On eviction the Ws. refused to go to their temporary accommodation provided by the local authority, and the whole family went to live with Mr W.'s mother in very grossly overcrowded conditions. The hospital psychiatric social worker and a caseworker from a voluntary family casework agency had been trying to help the family for some time. They had prevented eviction on a previous occasion by making strong representations to the landlord, but this time they had been taken by surprise, since the Ws. had assured them that the rent was up-to-date. After a short period with Mr W.'s mother the parents applied to the children's department for the children to be taken into care. The children's department arranged a meeting between the social workers concerned. As a result of fairly long discussions it was agreed that the children should be admitted to care. The social workers who knew the family well were anxious that the family relationships should be preserved and recommended that the children be placed in a small family group home.

The social workers then held a joint meeting with Mr and Mrs W. and Mr W.'s mother, who had been finding the children too great a burden and had written to the doctor in charge of the day hospital urging him to take some action. Plans for the future were discussed with the parents and arrangements were made to admit the children to a family group home. This seemed acceptable to the parents, who went out and bought each child a set of new clothes to go away with. However, the day before the children were due to leave their grandmother's home Mr W. was adamant that they were not going to leave him – he was their father and no one could force him to send his children away. He thought that if they went from him this time, he would never see them back again. This was discussed with him by the child care officer, and Mr W. seemed more satisfied. The children were taken to the home the following day with Mr W. and he seemed very pleased with it. It was explained that the parents could visit when they wished, provided that they gave the home some notice.

Some six weeks later the child care officer was visiting the home and was told that the parents were visiting, but without giving any notice. This had meant on one or two occasions that their children had not been in when they called. Mr W. when he had seen the children had told them that they would be getting a house soon, and this had made the children entertain unrealistic hopes for the future. The child care officer explained the family situation more fully to the residential staff and said she would contact Mr and Mrs W. to try to get them to see the importance of letting the home know when they were coming.

When the child care officer visited the Ws. she found only Mr W. at home. He expressed a great deal of hostility towards the local authority. All people did was to talk and make promises. He was particularly angry with the staff at the family group home, maintaining that they had promised to see that his children wrote to him every week. He had only had one letter and they had been there eight weeks: if he did not receive letters each week, he would stop paying money towards their upkeep. The child care officer tried to talk to him about how upset he felt about his children being away from him, but he was so angry that it was difficult to be sure he had heard what was said.

Three important points can be made in connection with this short description. First, we can see that the reasons for the reception of the children into care lie partly in the incapacity of the mother who is attending a day hospital, and partly in circumstances – the family was evicted. The social workers involved in the case had previously taken action to prevent eviction and, given more time, they would perhaps have tried to do this again. The nature of the action taken in the first instance is not clear, but increasingly social workers connected with child care are coming to appreciate that prevention often entails a very active 'campaign' on their part, both in connection with particular families and also with general features of the social environment which seem productive of social problems.

Second, the decision to take the children into care once it had been made was discussed carefully with the parents, and work had to be undertaken to help them to face the implications of the decision. In this case, work centred on Mr W., who clearly experienced very considerable pain at the separation from his children. 'Facing up to difficulties' cannot be achieved quickly, and we can see that whilst Mr W. did allow the children to leave home the issue of their separation from him will arise in many of his dealings with the family group home and with the children's department generally.

Third, the child care officer has the responsibility of ensuring that the children are receiving care appropriate to their needs. In the case of the W. children, this means that both the parents and the family group home staff are helped to understand the present situation. In trying to ensure good care for children, the child care officer is often in a position of a multiple interpreter helping parents and those caring for their children on a more temporary basis to interact with one another and with the children on a positive and fruitful basis.

Helping foster parents

The child care officer works with foster parents on an individual basis, but on occasions it is appropriate to work with groups of foster parents on a common range of problems. The following is a brief extract from one such meeting:

41

Group meeting of foster parents (Extract from middle of third meeting).

Mrs L.: I am sure these meetings mean a great deal to us, though [with a laugh] I know that my husband did not want to come at first. He thought that it would only be a lot of women gassing and that there wouldn't be any other men present.

Mr L.: [in a rather controlled manner] Perhaps it would be better if the mere males were allowed to speak for themselves. I admit that I was somewhat sceptical of these meetings. I have not had much contact with the C.C.O. who, as far as I can see, always came to my house when I was not there.

Mr P.: Well, I have always found the children's department very understanding.

Mrs P.: Yes, but what about the time when Peter [their foster child of 14] was staying out late and you thought he would have to go and the C.C.O. came, and you thought that what she said was just so much silly talk? I know you went on at me something awful.

Mrs C.: I'm not sure that we have come here to air our differences. After all we are doing a service to the community and I think that what husband and wife say to each other doesn't really come into it. Perhaps I am wrong, but at least that's what I think. Perhaps. . . .

Mr D.: Yes, why are we here? We've been coming for some weeks and Mrs L. may find it all right, because she can say things about her husband . . .

Mrs L.: I don't think you should. . . .

Mr D.: Oh, yes! It is the case and you cannot deny it. But all I wanted to say was that I am not sure why we are here at all. Perhaps we could have an answer. I hope I'm not being unpleasant, but perhaps the children's social worker could say what is the purpose of the meeting.

C.C.O.: I think that in the last few minutes we have experienced together a number of very important things. I think that we do sometimes wonder what we have let ourselves in for when we foster a child, and we sometimes experience the child as disturbing our own household, perhaps our own marriage. If this happens we may want to draw a line between those things that concern child care officer and those things which we think are not her business.

Mr P.: I don't think we want to get personal. I really haven't any complaints about the office or the officers who come. Maybe I don't always agree with them. Now, take Peter. We have had him now for four years. I will admit that I wasn't too keen on the idea at first. I don't think that men are. Fostering is much more for the women. At least that's what I always say, but there are times when the man has a special, I don't know, a special sort of part to play. That's when a boy, I mean when a boy is growing up, that's when . . . I'm not putting this very well.

C.C.O.: Perhaps one of the other fathers could say how they feel. I think that we are on to something very important.

Mrs L.: It's all very well having the man's point of view, but who has to bear the brunt of it? That's what I would like to know.

Mr D.: Well, I'd like to take up the point about what the fathers think. I can remember when I first heard about fostering from the wife.

Mrs L.: You see, it's the woman who brings it up.

Mr D.: Yes, I agree, but I did want to say what it felt like to me. I thought well somehow, as if it was a bit of a slap in the face.

Mrs C.: I think that's being a bit, I don't know, extreme. I think that it's all getting a bit deep for me. I

43

Mr D.:   don't know exactly what you think, Mrs D.?

Mr D.: Yes, but I think I know what Donald [Mr D.] means. I mean I think I would have liked to have more, I mean a bigger family. Yes.

Mr L.: But haven't we got to remember all the time that as foster parents we are second best? I think this is of some importance. You see, we mustn't get too emotionally involved. We cannot and should not try to take the place of the child's own parents. We must stay to some extent outside the picture. I hope I make myself clear.

Mrs L.: I'm not sure you can do this. I mean I'm not sure you can stay uninvolved. Isn't that really the job of the C.C.O. to stay on the edge and really watch what happens? I think we have to soldier on with the day to day worries and if we do that then we have to get into the picture, as you put it.

C.C.O.: I suppose that it must seem at the moment that I am 'on the edge of the picture', not very involved, while you all struggle on with the real problems.

Mrs C.: There you go again, taking it personally. I'm sure I don't have any such feelings. It really doesn't matter to me who comes to my house.

Mr D.: What I would like to ask is, whether the foster fathers shouldn't have a male visitor. I know my wife gets worked up before the visitor comes, whether the house is up to scratch, spick and span and all that. Now, I want someone to talk to, man-to-man. Not all this about the house. I want to talk to someone who knows what's what.

In this extract from the records of a group meeting of foster parents, it is possible to see the social worker helping those in a fostering situation to express their feelings and views about it, so that they will be better able to come to

44

terms with them. The group in the particular phase we have been watching seem to be concerned with a number of issues that are of central importance in fostering. The work of the child care officer or of any social worker concerned with a fostering programme is to help foster parents with them. These problems include those concerning their identity as foster parents, and their value (see Mr L.'s remark about 'second best'), and also their relationship with the children's department and the child care officer (how far was the social worker really understanding what they felt and how far did her job entail 'prying into' what some of the group felt were private matters between husband and wife?).

MEDICAL SOCIAL WORK

Most medical social workers work in hospitals, though an increasing number are employed helping sick and disabled people who manage to live 'normal' lives in the community. On 30 September 1967 there were 1,684 social workers and assistants in hospitals of whom 1,040 were professionally qualified. Sickness and disability concern the social worker for a number of reasons. Sometimes the cure of the sickness depends upon factors in the patient's social environment: the sick person may be slow in recovering because he is worried about money, his relationship with his children, or his job. As one patient said in a recent small enquiry into consumer reaction to medical social work:[3] 'I found it a relief to discuss with the social worker my angry feelings about the operation and my fears that this would have an adverse effect on my relationship with my husband.' On other occasions, worry enters into the original medical condition and becomes as it were, part of the illness. Thus, another patient in the same study commented: 'I had a very bad confinement and lost all memory of it. I felt frightened and wanted to go home. The doctors said that this would be suicide, and asked the medical social worker to see me. I talked to her about being worried. She was sympathetic and comforting, and when I was ready to go home, arranged help.' Within the hospital the medical social worker is often seen as someone from the medical staff with whom the patients can discuss aspects of their life and treatment in the hospital that they would otherwise not reveal. 'The medical social worker is independent of the rest of the hospital. Acts as a go-between. If patients feel awkward with the medical or nursing staff, they need to talk to the social worker. The medical social worker needs to belong to the hospital and to the community outside.'

Treatment in hospital often presents patients and their families with something in the nature of a crisis. This may be because the illness carries a particular significance for them and for others in their society (e.g., cancer), because the illness and its treatment will deprive the family of one of its key members for a long period of time, and because of the effects of the actual experience on the patient. One example of the kind of crisis that may be encountered is given in the following case:

> *Mr K*. Mr K. is aged forty, and was employed as a foreman in a firm manufacturing printing machines. His wife is thirty-nine, and they have four girls of whom the youngest, aged five, is a mongol. Mr K. was admitted to a teaching hospital in the north of England for operative treatment for thyrotoxicosis. The initial treatment consisted of medication to enable the rate of thyroid metabolism to slow down sufficiently to allow the operation. After three days in hospital he was referred to the medical social worker by the ward sister, because he was very restless and unhappy in the ward.

The medical social worker went to see Mr K. on the ward. He did not appear very pleased to see her and wanted to know why she had come. The medical social worker said the ward sister had thought he was not settling in too well, and she had wondered if anything was bothering him. She explained that the medical social work department was there to help with any worries people might have. Mr K. said that in that case it was simple: he had no problems. He and his wife were coping very well, and they were very independent

46

people. The medical social worker asked, 'In what way, independent? Perhaps you could explain a little?' Mr K. paused, and then said how it had been the same when their youngest had been born – lots of people coming and saying they would help but he and his wife managed; they had to. The medical social worker then helped Mr K. to talk more about his experiences at that time and about his contacts then with doctors. It gradually became clear that Mr K. had two main problems in relation to his present medical care. First, he had a considerable amount of guilt in connection with his mongol child and a great deal of this was expressed in terms of anger and hostility towards the doctors for their inability to change his daughter's condition. Second, he laid very great stress on his independence and this appeared to mask a fear, roused by his temporary withdrawal from work, that he would in fact become very dependent as a result of his stay in the hospital. This fear was partly the result of the fact that he worked very long hours in order to avoid some of the pressing emotional problems at home. By seeing him daily the medical social worker was able to help him to make good use of his medication period before the operation, during which it was essential that he should be as little troubled by worry as possible.

THE PROBATION SERVICE

The three main functions of the probation after-care service have recently been described as: 'Social investigations and diagnosis; providing a non-institutional means of preventing recidivism (the condition of being a chronic offender and prisoner) and providing a referral agency and a social casework service for those other cases where, in the extremity of social breakdown, the intervention of the court is required and sought'.[4] These are very far-ranging functions and in this section only one will be illustrated from the records of a social worker, namely social investigation and diagnosis.

The case concerns a fifty-two-year-old woman accused of shop-lifting, and we can see from the probation officer's report the way in which a social enquiry can begin to illuminate an initially puzzling situation.

Report for the Magistrates Court 13 February 1968

Concerning:
Mrs Amelia Jane S., aged 52

Address:	3, The Close, S.
Born:	13 1 1906. Religion: C. of E.
Family:	
Husband:	Mr Charles S., aged 63. Bank Manager
Concerned:	Mrs Amelia S. Housewife
Son:	Mr Frank S., aged 32. Doctor. Married and living in Canada
Son:	Mr John S., aged 28. Architect. Married and living in Scotland
Daughter:	Miss Joan S., aged 19. University student
Charge:	Shop-lifting from self-service stores in S. . . . I understand that Mrs S. is asking for similar offences to be taken into consideration.

Home and financial circumstances

Mr and Mrs S. have lived in their present house for the past fifteen years, having moved here from London when Mr S. was appointed to the local branch of X Bank. They own the house, which has five bedrooms and a large garden and which is very comfortable and well kept. They have no financial problems and Mrs S. says that on each occasion when she took goods from shops, she had more than sufficient money in her handbag to pay for them.

Circumstances of the offences

Mrs S. is at a loss to understand her own behaviour. Not only had she sufficient money to pay for the goods she took, but she took things for which she had no use at all,

48

such as strained baby foods and tinned milk, which neither she nor her husband like. She is exceedingly distressed by her behaviour and horrified at the forthcoming court appearance and the possibility of publicity, which may damage her own and her husband's reputation.

Personal history

Mrs S. is the only daughter of an army officer and spent her childhood constantly on the move, following her father's postings. She wanted to become a nurse when she left school, but her parents were opposed to the idea and Mrs S. did a secretarial training. She still feels disappointed at not being allowed to do nursing. While training she met her husband and after a brief engagement they were married, when Mrs S. was nineteen. Their first child was born a year later.

Mrs S. describes her married life as happy and she enjoyed her children and found satisfaction in caring for them. She lost a baby girl at birth, after the birth of her second son and tells me she was depressed for a time, but became better after the family moved to X, where she made friends easily and settled into the village life. This was helped by the fact that her parents were living in a village some ten miles away, and Mrs S. renewed her contact with them and particularly with her mother, of whom she saw a great deal until her death last year. Mrs S. says she and her husband have always got on well and shared similar interests in outdoor pursuits, in the children and in entertaining.

Mrs S.'s health was good until last year when she fell and broke an ankle. This has proved difficult to mend and she has been restricted in her movements recently.

Conclusions

It seems that Mrs S. has suffered a number of losses recently. Her mother died last year and shortly after that Mrs S. broke her ankle and could no longer accompany her husband on walks or garden with him. At much the same time her eldest son emigrated to Canada with his three children, of whom Mrs S. had been seeing a good deal, and her daughter left home for the first time. Mrs S. herself is not aware of being depressed, although she says the future seems very uninteresting and she no longer finds any comfort in religion. She told me her useful days are over and the best thing the court can do is to send her to prison.

I would respectfully suggest that Mrs S. is reacting to a series of losses. Should the court wish to consider a probation order, I think Mrs S. would be able to make use of support. If the court requires a psychiatric report Mrs S. is willing to see a psychiatrist.

P.G.

Probation Officer.

A GENERAL QUESTION: IS SOCIAL WORK ALWAYS THE SAME?

We have examined and discussed briefly a number of illustrations of social work in a variety of different organizational settings. Sometimes they seem to be concerned at least in part with the same problems (e.g., the mentally subnormal child of Mr and Mrs R. and the mongol child of Mr K.), and often they seem to illustrate social workers behaving in approximately the same way. How significant is this? Does it indicate that social work is very much the same kind of activity wherever it is practised, and that the organizational 'setting' has only a minimal influence on both the social worker and the client? These are significant questions, and in the attempt at least to begin to answer them we can extend our ideas about the nature of social work.

It is apparent that there are common elements in the practice of social work in the different organizational settings. As we have seen the social worker is often involved in trying to help people to use a particular service and to get the most benefit out of their contact with it. Yet it is not the case that helping a person to use the child guidance clinic, in spite of the fact that she fears that by so doing she might agree with the medical authorities that her child is 'mad', is quite the same as assisting an old person to use the local authority services even though she is convinced that to do so is a way of accepting 'charity'. There are obvious similarities between these two instances, and also differences important enough to, as it were, 'get into' the working relationship between client and social worker. Whether or not the differences are sufficient to necessitate a functional division of labour between the social workers concerned is, of course, another question.

It is partly answered by enquiring to what extent social workers in different fields require different knowledge and the extent to which they can be seen as applying differentially the same theories and concepts. Consider the following examples of attempts to argue the case that a common framework can readily be applied to the problems encountered by social workers in their different fields. First, in relation to knowledge, it has been suggested that separation is a psychological process that can occur in different situations, even though its nature is always the same. So that whilst a social worker in the field of child care will be concerned with arranging a child's separation from, say a foster home, and with helping the child to cope with this, it is also true to say that workers in other fields are equally involved in the separation process. The child care worker needs to know about separation, but 'What about the separation factor in the school phobia? In prolonged parental illness? In desertion by a parent? In divorce? In death?'[5] These problems might well be dealt with in different kinds of social agency and by social workers bearing different names. Are they all, agencies and workers, involved with the same separation process? There are two general answers to this type of question. One would suggest that whilst a child separating from his mother does not represent the same problem as a recently bereaved widow learning to deal with separation from her dead husband, there is none the less enough similarity to make it a matter more or less of indifference which agency and which social worker deals with which client. The second approach would be to argue that each field of social work has something like a psychology of its own. Thus, one author argues that in social work there is a generic psychology concerned with taking help and in addition each field 'does have a psychology of its own'. 'Each field of practice, or service, is recognized as having its own body of knowledge and its own 'psychology' which the worker must make his own and integrate in his helping skill as he moves from field of practice to field of practice.'[6]

Each position has certain assets. The first draws attention to interesting similarities between problems which might otherwise remain unconnected. The second suggests that we should attend more closely to what each agency is 'saying' to its particular clientele, not simply through the social worker, but through its organizational climate and its place and significance in the community.

The decision on which answer to accept is not one that has so far been settled by any kind of investigation, though most social workers have decided against the latter approach.

The second example of an attempt to apply a common framework to social work can be found in a recent treatment of the question of 'authority'.

Studt suggests that in fact all social workers use authority, not simply those working in fields that were once classed as specially 'authority-based', like probation:

> The public welfare worker acts with authority when he determines eligibility; the group worker uses authority in refusing to permit certain behaviour in the clubroom; the child welfare worker is authoritative in selecting a foster home; the school social worker represents the authority of the State in insisting with child and family that he must attend school; the therapist in the clinic exercises authority in setting the conditions for treatment.[7]

In all these examples, it is suggested, the social worker is primarily engaged in defining certain aspects of the client's role which must be accepted if he is to participate in the service. 'Most authority actions are simply a matter of making explicit, in a behavioural context, the role definitions governing the subordinate position.' Yet we can still ask in which ways the exercise of authority is 'the same' in the instances quoted. If we ask how a client can in each of these instances question 'authority', in the case of an adverse decision, we begin to see some of the ways in which the situations differ from each other. We have in fact to recognize that 'authority' cannot be 'applied' to a range of situations as if there were universal agreement about its meaning. There seem in fact to be two general approaches. One defines authority simply as 'legitimized' power, but the other stresses the sentiments of those over whom authority is exercised. In this latter meaning authority is never given, but is always contingent upon its exercise. Its exercise is obviously something that will depend on the particular occasion. This is not to say that generalizations about the exercise of authority by social workers may not be possible, but much generalization must be based on empirical observations rather than theoretical assumptions of a rather abstract kind.

Specific strains

In thinking about the organization in which social workers are employed we also need to investigate the extent to which social workers are able, psychologically, to bear the strains that remain specially associated with particular kinds of work. It is possible that this may be one of the sources from which future specialization may grow. The Seebohm Committee considered this argument, but rejected it, without much by way of justification, in favour of an attempt 'to meet all the social needs of the family or individual together and as a whole'. To achieve this, they argued,

> It is essential that the family or individual should be the concern of one social worker with a comprehensive approach to the social problems of his clients. It follows that a single worker, and through him the social service department as a whole, can be held accountable for the standard of care the family or individual receives (or fails to receive) much more easily than if responsibility is fragmented between several workers.

Accountability is of considerable importance, but a service must also satisfy other equally important criteria. It must for example be psychologically and organizationally feasible. To what extent can we identify some of the different functions that a general purpose department must serve and the stresses and strains consequent upon them.

Any new organization must continue to provide services for deprived children and for the mentally ill in the community. Each of these functions carries with it a different set of strains, and a different set of working problems which might act as challenge and stimulus. The children's worker, for example, must be prepared to act to remove children from home and to help to provide substitute care. The social worker dealing with the sick and the ill must come to terms with a range of emotional and intellectual problems concerned with authoritative medicine, with mutilation, cure and failure, permanent harm, death. Each of these problems may not be well handled by other personnel concerned and this increases the responsibility of the social worker. Take an example from the hospital field, namely the way in which death is 'handled'. This is obviously a subject that many workers in the hospital find very difficult, and towards which they adopt various defensive measures, some of which have unfortunate results for patients and their families. A recent hospital study in America concluded that

A patient who was terminally ill created crises in human relations for those who were caring for him. One dilemma arose from the fact that not every member of the group involved – the sick person, the spouse, the responsible physician, nurses, and other family members – realized the illness was a fatal one. It may have been in the interests of some persons to mislead other members of the group. Evasions, silences, half-truths, and deliberate lies then became elements in the social realities that tied the group together, and, in turn, influences the communications of one person with another. A second dilemma arose from the lack of explicit norms in our culture to guide the day-to-day relations of the group as death approached. A third revolved around the uncertainty of when death would occur.[9]

A social worker in a hospital must act within contexts of this kind, and must be able to understand and bear the stress arising not simply from the patient's condition, nor just from other hospital staff, nor from wider cultural attitudes, but from the interaction of all three.

Whether we emphasize the generic aspects of social work or its specialized aspects arising from work with particular groups or in particular fields, it is important to identify the stresses and the rewards attached to particular functions and also the impact particular organizational settings may have on the client. Field workers and those administering the services must be concerned that as many resources as possible are brought to bear on the complex social problems that they are trying to solve. We neglect one significant resource if we do not attend to what can best be described as the 'fit' or lack of 'fit' between social worker, agency and client.

NOTES

[1] *Community Work and Social Change*, London: Longmans, for the General Studies Association, 1968.

[2] *Report* of the (Seebohm) Committee on Local Authority and Allied Personal Services, Cmnd. 3703, S. 455, 1968.

[3] Butrym, Z. *Medical Social Work in Action*, Bell & Son, 1968.

[4] 'The Place of the Probation and After Care Service in Judicial Administration'. Report of the Principal Probation Officers' Conference, April 1968.

[5] Hollis, F., 'The Generic and Specific in Social Casework Re-examined', *Social Casework*, May 1956.

[6] Smalley, R., *Theory for Social Work Practice*, New York: Columbia University Press, 1967, p. 158.

[7] Studt, E., 'Worker-Client Authority Relationships in Social Work', *Social Work (U.S.A.)*, January, 1959.

[8] *Report* of the (Seebohm) Committee, op. cit.

[9] Duff, R. S. & Hollingshead, H. B., *Sickness and Society*, New York: Harper & Row, 1968, Chapter 15, 'Dying and Death'.

3

Social Work Knowledge

IT IS DIFFICULT to set bounds to the knowledge any one kind of professional should have. In social work, for example, it seems it is always possible, and hence not very useful, to say that social workers should know more about this or that phenomenon.[1] Social workers at present often seem to entertain unlimited expectations of the advances likely to be made as a result of collaboration between the social worker and the social scientist, and it seems frequently to be assumed that the social worker is, or should be, knowledgeable about every subject from the latest housing legislation to cultural variations on an Oedipal theme. Yet at the same time there is a strong vein of scepticism running through much modern social work which stubbornly questions the exclusive faith placed in theoretical knowledge. In 1897 C. S. Loch admitted that 'A friend and critic of the Society [the Charity Organization Society] once set me thinking, by saying abruptly: "It's all very well for you to read and study. But you know the members of your committees don't. They plod along with their cases: but you are quite wrong, if you think they are troubling themselves about general causes, principles or any wider questions".'[2] Loch admitted that he was forced to agree with much of this argument. It represents a kind of factual scepticism: social workers in fact take little note of theoretical speculation. There is also a normative scepticism which suggests that social workers are right to be thus negligent. 'Academic persons', states an Annual Report of the Charity Organization Society, 'select a hypothesis and build plans and practice upon it. Feeling, willing, hoping, fearing, suffering human beings are expected to conform. The C.O.S. arrives at its theory and practice by the opposite method. They sprang up vivid and alive in the course of their fireside chats. . . .'[3] That scepticism of one kind or the other is still strong, can be illustrated from a work more recently published:

> The only advice that anyone can give the worker is that he should learn all he can in abstract ways about relationships in general, the settings in which they should take place, the levels of intensity they should or should not include, check what he has learned in this way with his own experience, accept and reject what he will, forget all about it, and then relax and allow things to happen.[4]

This kind of interpretation of the relationship between knowledge and practice in social work requires much more study than it has so far received. Instead of advancing claims – as we have in social work – for the exercise of professional authority derived from social work knowledge, we could more profitably have attended to attempting to understand phenomena within reach of our own experience: for example, the different ways in which the teachers and the practitioners of social work view the relationship between knowledge and practice.

There seem to be three main elements that require understanding. First, social work practitioners are wary of generalization. It could be argued that this wariness is bound up with a deep theoretical conviction about the importance of 'the individual': 'If the individual is lost all is lost,' wrote a nineteenth-century social worker.[5] It is also connected with a view of the inevitable shortcoming of any generalization. This was well expressed by S. R. Bosanquet early in the nineteenth century, but it is an attitude that persists to the present:

Neither idleness, nor vice, nor the unequal division of property, nor want of education, nor all these together, nor a hundred more than these, are the causes of all the poverty which exists; no one can tell, or ascertain, or guess at all, all the causes from which poverty arises. Every such pretension must be defeated by the next day's investigation; and any general rules by which we may bind ourselves must work injustice, and will be more and more defeated by a wider and more impartial experience.[6]

Much the same distrust of generalization is to be found in the more recent statement that 'effective casework service is not a matter of following rules nor can it be secured through the possession of theoretical knowledge'.[7] What these two statements have in common seems to be the belief that a generalization or a general rule are somehow by their nature restricting rather than, at least partially, liberating. If a generalization can be said to hold over a particular area there are some points at which one's social work can be anchored. Social work is not *just* a matter of following rules or simply something that follows, as it were, from theoretical knowledge, but this does not allow us to neglect the particular contribution of rules or knowledge.

Whilst many practitioners have been in the past sceptical of knowledge and some remain so today, there are others who see theoretical knowledge as a useful summary of what they have already learned the hard, and for some perhaps the only, way. It represents simply and only a record of their own experience. This is well illustrated in the comments of a highly placed welfare administrator replying to an early questionnaire on the value of sociology as a pre-vocational subject for social workers. She began by commenting on the great value of personal experience: 'I came to know the servant problem by being a servant. . . . At the age of 47 I took one course in social psychology under Professor Mead at the University of Chicago. It was interesting as a trip in an aeroplane would be to a person who had walked over the area and knew every road and path by heart.'[8] The reply of another senior social worker to the same enquiry illustrates a different position, namely that theoretical knowledge often speaks with barely a whisper to the pressing practical concerns of the social worker. Thus, Porter Lee, who later became one of the leading American social work teachers of his period, replied:

> So far as I can see now, it has been no earthly use to me to know how Aristotle or Plato or Knox or anybody else, met the daily task with which they were confronted. What I am interested in, is how I am going to take care of Bill Smith and his family of sick or neglected children, or how I am going to assist in securing more adequate or more sensible care and control of the feeble minded, and many other questions of almost equal importance.[9]

SOURCES OF KNOWLEDGE

At present emphasis is given to the value of empirical and scientific research as the source of social work knowledge. As the Seebohm Report stated, 'The personal social services are large-scale experiments in ways of helping those in need. It is both wasteful and irresponsible to set experiments in motion and omit to record and analyse what happens. . . . More effective personal social services mean making better decisions about how to assist individuals and families, and better decisions depend upon better information.'[10] Such sources of knowledge are of crucial importance, and as such they will be discussed later in this section, but we should also examine what is often described as the practical knowledge or wisdom of any profession. The practical wisdom of the practitioner requires more study than it has received. It constitutes a range of abilities that are essential, but they need to be criticized and assessed because of their unstable nature. By this I mean that our ideas about so many aspects of our society are changing quite rapidly (e.g., about language) and, besides, we cannot be sure, because of the comparative youth of social work, whether it is to be seen as an applied science or a kind of moralizing. Whichever seems to us the more important, we must not overstress, say, the idea of applied science so that we restrict the sources from which we derive our insights. We must not think that it is only 'scientific studies' that will inform the training of the social worker. Two examples from literature will show the kinds of insight we are likely to derive from 'non-scientific' sources. The first is from the nineteenth-century writer Emerson, and concerns what a social worker might call 'the problem of giving financial help'. Emerson's essay on 'Gifts' suggests economically many of the problems that arise in the interchange of gifts and money in our society:

> The law of benefits is a difficult channel, which requires careful sailing. . . . We wish to be self-sustained. We do not quite forgive a giver. The hand that feeds us is in some danger of being bitten. We can receive anything from love, for that is a way of receiving it from ourselves; but not from *anyone* who assumes to bestow. We sometimes hate the meat which we eat, because there seems something of degrading dependence in living by it.[11]

The second example comes from much earlier times and contributes an important idea in connection with what a social worker might describe as the causation of delinquency or perhaps of deviance in general. It is taken from the *Confessions* of St Augustine. St Augustine in the following passage is attempting to discover why he stole some pears:

> . . . it was not the pears that my unhappy soul desired. I had plenty of my own, better than those, and I only picked them so that I might steal. For no sooner had I picked them, than I threw them away, and I tasted nothing in them but my own sin, which I relished and enjoyed. If any part of those pears passed my lips, it was the sin that gave it flavour. . . . What was it, then, that pleased me in that act of theft? . . . Could I enjoy doing wrong for no other reason than that it was wrong?[12]

Such insights as these are valuable: they are part of the practical knowledge people acquire as they live in their society. This practical knowledge should not be undervalued, but at the same time we must recognize that it derives from a particular social position which the person in question holds – it is always more or less partial knowledge. It, thus, constitutes for the social worker a helpful beginning rather than an arrival point with which he can be satisfied. Thus, the idea that Emerson is seeking to convey of the responses evoked in those receiving gifts, services, etc., from others, seems to fit with what we can see of our present society, and it is certainly a notion that the social worker has for some time been trained to accept. Yet, it should be subjected to critical scrutiny. One such attempt has been made by an American social work teacher, Bertha Reynolds.[13] At one stage of her career she worked as a social worker for a seamen's union, and later wrote a book expressing the different quality of social work undertaken with people who, because they were members of the union, felt they had a right to the social service provided by the union. Reynolds in one chapter asks simply, 'Must it hurt to be helped?' She recorded her belief that at least amongst the working class, giving and taking were very normal aspects of daily living, taken for granted as 'natural'. Why, then should some people experience such difficulty in approaching the conventional social work agency? Her answer was that people dislike offers of help that may create obligations whose nature is very unclear. In other words, they suspect 'something for nothing', either because the 'something' will turn out to be 'nothing' or because the 'nothing' that will be demanded of them will turn out to contain serious obligations. It does not hurt to be helped if you feel you belong, but it does hurt if by the act of receiving help, you are relegated to the status of a child or a permanently handicapped person.

Again, this argument seems plausible, but we should note that it is based on the impressionistic record of experience. We need many more such records, but only because they produce likely ideas that must be subjected to the further test of empirical investigation. As the first chapter suggested, we are only at the very beginning of factual enquiry about the views recipients hold about the service they receive.

Knowledge of what?

Many attempts have been made to list the various kinds of knowledge required by the social worker. In 1929 an important conference in America[14] suggested the following general items:

1. Knowledge of typical deviations from accepted standards of social life;
2. Use of norms of human life and human relationships;
3. The significance of social history as the basis for particularizing the human being in need;
4. Established methods of study and treatment of human beings in need;
5. Use of established community resources in social treatment;
6. Adaptation of scientific knowledge and formulations of experience to the requirements of social casework;
7. Consciousness of a philosophy which determines the purposes, ethics and obligations of social casework;
8. The blending of the foregoing into social treatment.

These were considered to form the core of knowledge essential for any social caseworker, and there were in addition special items of knowledge required for practice in a particular field. For example, in the practice of family casework, the social worker was required to know the minimum essentials for keeping a family together, the effect of migrancy, and to have, amongst other skills, an ability to deal with the psychology of enforced idleness. Soon after this Karpf[15] stated that social workers needed to have the following intellectual equipment: a knowledge of backgrounds, a philosophy of life and a point of view, a knowledge of human nature, a knowledge of norms, clarity and accuracy of thought. In addition each of the social sciences could make a contribution to social work: 'Without the hope and courage which the theories of social causation and social control give, no one could long endure social work.' More recent tendencies have been to simplify the knowledge required under three main headings of human growth and behaviour, the social influences on behaviour, and the social services. These headings will be used in the following discussion, but it is worth making some general points on the lists of requirements so far produced. First, only one of these (Karpf) is based on empirical study of social work records. This deficiency needs to be remedied since there often seems to be a considerable discrepancy between what a social worker appears to do for and with her clients, and the reasonably complex kinds of knowledge apparently required for the effective operation of social work. Second, some of the knowledge required seems to be very difficult to acquire. There are perhaps two main kinds of difficulty: being sufficiently sure of the 'facts' (e.g., about normal and abnormal behaviour) because in so many aspects of social life, description and evaluation are inextricably inter-mingled; and, doubts about when it can justifiably be claimed that the 'knowledge' has been obtained. For example, it would be generally agreed that the stress on a 'philosophy of life' sounded correct on roughly common-sense grounds, but what counts as such a philosophy and will any philosophy of life be adequate – for instance, one that supported extremes of inequality? Third, there seems to have been a tendency to move away from a too specific delineation of the knowledge required. This is partly because we do not, for example, know 'the minimum essentials for keeping a family together', and partly because such knowledge as that of the psychology of enforced idleness is now seen as part of a much wider, though still imperfectly appreciated, psychology and sociology of work.

Human growth and behaviour

Just as earlier ideas about the importance of 'background' did less than justice to the essential idea that men and their environment are in continual and dynamic interaction, so the separation of human growth and behaviour from the social influences on behaviour may have unhelpful reper-cussions. Talking of social influences *on* behaviour may suggest that behaviour is, as it were, going on, and that at certain points social influences (seen as somehow not the behaviour of others) impinge on it from the outside. This is not a satisfactory perspective on human behaviour, but the separate consideration of human growth and behaviour and the social influences on behaviour perhaps helps us to reduce to more manageable proportions the considerable and growing mass of material that could be discussed.

The social worker's self knowledge

Mary Richmond was of the opinion that the social worker 'must have a conception of the possibilities of human nature – of the suggestibility, improvability, and supreme value of folks. . . . What he thinks of human nature is bounded by what he knows of human nature, and what he knows in this field is bounded by what he is'.[16] This reference to the social worker himself draws attention to the fact that the knowledge a social worker requires of 'human nature' includes self-knowledge. This has been emphasized since social work and psychoanalysis were brought into close, if not systematic relationship after the beginning of the specialization of psychiatric social work. It is now sometimes suggested that too much emphasis is given to this, but provided self-awareness is seen in both a psychological and a sociological framework it does seem to constitute an essential part of a social worker's equipment. By sociological self-awareness I mean that 'The life of an individual cannot be adequately understood without reference to the institutions within which his biography is enacted.'[17]

Given this safeguard, self-awareness is essential for the social worker. Why is this so? First, it constitutes a kind of protection for the client. Self-awareness is not so much a state of knowledge arrived at once and for all, but rather an attitude of mind that is prepared to consider the extent to which any particular outcome of social work action at a certain point in time may be the result of unhelpful and negative response on the part of the social worker. These responses may have a number of different sources, but one of the most important is likely to be the social worker's own

64

previous development. It may be, for example, that because of his experiences in his childhood he is liable to react over-positively to clients who are battling against authority. Thus, self-awareness helps to expose features of the handling of a situation which may result in the client receiving less service than he should. In other words, self-awareness helps to achieve one of the most important aims of a social service, namely that within the terms of eligibility it should be given on a universalistic basis. By this I mean that extraneous factors (such as the social worker's difficulty in forming reasonably good relationships with a particular group – for example, the parents of cruelly treated children) should not enter into the decision about helping nor, as far as possible, into the process of help. Help is available in terms of need rather than of such particular features of the client as colour, religion or behavioural characteristics.

Second, self-awareness helps the social worker to achieve a position which might be described as one of strong, involved neutrality. It may well, for example, be important to give the client who, so to speak, comes spoiling for a fight a sounding board rather than retaliation in kind or, alternatively, a feather bed. In developing self-awareness we help to avoid two extreme kinds of reaction. The first is simply a complementary response to whatever behaviour we are witnessing. This is a response of like to like (anger to anger, dejection to dejection). The second response is a too ready attempt to correct the behaviour. We may thus attempt to 'cheer' the depressed without letting the extent of his depression be experienced by the worker. Or we may attempt to define too quickly and too precisely the worry that the client has. Thus, a nurse, who had been told that she must attend to the anxieties of her patients was unable to tolerate the uncertainty of one of them who seemed to be very unsure of her problem. 'What,' the nurse roundly enquired, 'what precisely is your anxiety?' Here we see that the nurse's inability to tolerate uncertainty contributed to making it much more difficult for the patient to express a rather boundless anxiety.

Third, self-awareness helps the social worker by adding

to her ability to understand situations: it adds a further dimension. The social worker has to understand very complex situations and sometimes she gains an insight into what is going on by attending to the feelings aroused in herself by the situation. By reflecting on them, she can sometimes begin to see what she might be expected to feel. A great deal of our activity is purposive: we try much of the time to make other people behave towards us in particular ways – to see us in a particular light, to notice some aspect of our behaviour, to be dependent, angry, and so on. So, in attending to the feelings we experience at a particular time we often have the opportunity to apprehend the purpose that other people entertain towards us. It is for this reason that the maxim in social work makes sense: Listen not to what someone is saying but to what they are trying to tell.

But the social worker's self-knowledge is part of his knowledge of 'human nature'. This term has been put in inverted commas since we are now very much more diffident than we used to be concerning statements about human nature. We are much more aware of the importance of 'background factors' and also of some of the difficulties in putting forward a reasonable account of human growth and development. The subject is extremely wide-ranging and the student of social work easily recognizes this when faced with the requirements that, in the words of a recent specification:

> . . . the social worker must have some knowledge of human growth and development in both its physiological and psychological aspects throughout the chief phases of the life cycle from birth to old age and death. He must be aware of the basic human drives and of the significance of the social relationships into which individuals enter especially in their family unit. He must know sufficient about health and disease to recognize, and have some understanding of, variation within the normal as well as deviations, particularly as manifested in mental and physical handicaps, mental illness, 'problem' family living and unmarried parenthood.[18]

66

It is perhaps not surprising that social workers are often criticized for seeming to make claims to omniscience.

Two specific aspects of the range of problems presented by the requirement 'to know about' human growth and behaviour have been selected for illustration, since they show both the complexity and the promise of this part of a social work course. We shall consider learning about one particular element in human behaviour, sex-typed behaviour, and one way of organizing our knowledge that seems to suggest interesting possibilities for the future.

Sex-typed behaviour

Sex differences in behaviour appear very early in the life of the individual. In animal studies – and reference to this valuable source of ideas indicates the wide range of material that has come to be used in the consideration of human behaviour – male infants show a much greater inclination than the female for aggressive play. In studies of different types of monkeys and great apes, the young female shows, in contrast to the male, more interest in infants and in grooming behaviour. Several studies of newborn human babies suggest some very early differentiation in behaviour between males and females. For instance, it has been observed that females of two to three months are more responsive to skin exposure than newborn males of the same age. As children grow up their patterns of behaviour become increasingly differentiated. How can this be explained? It clearly is an aspect of fundamental importance to those seeking to understand human development.

The answer can be sought through a number of different approaches: stress can be placed on the genetic, the cognitive or the life-experience factors. Some, for instance, would argue that the child is, as it were, sexually 'neutral' at birth and that thereafter he learns his gender, selecting the appropriate repertoire of behaviour. Others argue from a more general position that there is little evidence that cognitive changes in opinions, beliefs or values produce behaviour change, and, more particularly, that a child attains sexual identity on the basis of previously learned behaviour. Other writers stress the way in which a child learns sex-typed behaviour in the process of socialization, but this is a very complex process and it is often difficult to see how different socialization practices which parents direct to boys and to girls produce the outcome we perceive in sex-typed behaviour. For instance, in a study of differences in the reactions of mothers and fathers to aggression and dependency behaviour in male and female children, mothers were found to be more permissive to both kinds of behaviour in their sons, while fathers were more permissive of the behaviour in their daughters.[19] Another study suggested that daughters of mothers who worked outside the home did not sex-type behaviour as much as daughters of non-working mothers.[20]

Now it would be possible to examine the considerable literature on the subject of sex-typed behaviour at some length, but the topic has been sufficiently introduced to enable us to grasp two important points about the teaching of human growth and behaviour. Firstly, the subject is extremely complex and it is difficult to come to firmly established and widely agreed conclusions about any major aspect. Secondly, this obvious fact poses a number of related problems to those concerned with social work education. The subject must not be taught as a series of discrete pieces of information about human conduct, if it is to constitute a form of understanding in contrast to what Dearden has recently called the 'rucksack theory of knowledge'.

> The 'rucksack' theory of knowledge is the theory that knowledge is just a jumbled mass of information such as might be exhibited to advantage on a quiz programme. The two revelant features in the analogy are that rucksacks can be more or less full, and that they are loosely carried behind. The knowledge embraced in a form of understanding, however, is organized, well-founded, and so ingrained in the mind as to transform, not just supply more information about, one's experience.[21]

But on what basis is such a form of understanding to be

organized? The social worker is, after all, preparing to act in, rather than to research into, the field of human behaviour. Two main answers to this question are offered at the present time. The first stresses scientific study as the basis, the second relies more heavily on a less systematic and more immediately experiential foundation.

Two recent articles on the teaching of human growth and behaviour can be used to illustrate the kind of distinction I have in mind. The first advocates[22] a scientific psychological approach on the grounds that it offers a possible basis for explaining, predicting and modifying human behaviour and that it also contains attitudes and values which may be desirable in social work practice. For example, the empirical basis of science (i.e. what is the evidence rather than 'who said it?'), the utilization of new knowledge and the assumption that all human behaviour is determined and lawful could all, it is argued, be usefully incorporated within social work. The second article starts from the assumption that the basis of social work is empathy and the social worker as such 'must be concerned with refining the capacity to perceive others' experiences and with conceptualizing them'. Confronted with such a task, however, the social worker has no long-standing formal tradition to which to look for help. In this case the social work teacher has to establish his or her own methods, using intellectual traditions where appropriate, but not feeling bound to copy any one of them directly and exactly. The teacher of human growth and behaviour is faced with a number of competing general theories, and the author suggests that it is a useful procedure to present the student with several theories of personality, but unless the student has 'had the opportunity to explore the concrete instances of his experience of human being, then these theories will be inert ideas to him, and in this case they can only form the basis for sterile argument unrelated to life'.[23]

Stages of development

The notion of progression through a series of stages of

human development is not without its difficulties (e.g., can we identify the stages sufficiently to be sure of the differences between them?). But it seems to offer a useful manner of organizing the innumerable theories, facts and impressions that characterize the subject of human growth and behaviour. In this section one of the more recent developments of this approach will be examined. It is an approach that represents an advance on previous orientations which tended to see the stages in terms of individual interior psychological development, rather than a combination of individual and inter-personal factors. It also represents the growing conviction that personality continues to develop after the early years of childhood. The 'crises' of marriage and pregnancy and even old age often present opportunities for further development on the part of the individual personality.

The approach we are considering suggests that we examine human development in terms of a series of critical transitions from one role to another which always involve the responses of other people, and cognitive and adaptive processes. Take marriage as an example of a critical role transition. This has recently been analysed by Rapoport[24] into a series of related tasks imposed on and undertaken by the individual in relation to his own personality and his interpersonal relations. Marriage is divided by Rapoport, into a number of phases – engagement, honeymoon and early marriage. Following her discussion enables us to see some of the results to be obtained from this general approach. It seems, for instance, to enable the student of social work to make some detailed and meaningful statements about any particular marriage:

Engagement transition tasks

Personal

1. Developing a capacity for accepting the emotional responsibilities of marriage

Interpersonal

1. Establishing a 'couple' identity

Personal

2. Developing a capacity for accepting the material responsibilities of marriage
3. Developing a pattern of gratification compatible with the expectations and needs of the partner

Interpersonal

2. Developing a mutually satisfactory sexual adjustment for the engagement period
3. Developing a mutually satisfactory orientation to family planning
4. Establishing a mutually satisfactory system of pair communication
5. Establishing a mutually satisfactory pattern of external relations
6 Developing mutually satisfactory patterns of work and of leisure
7. Establishing a mutually satisfactory pattern in regard to wedding plans and the early months of marriage
8. Establishing mutually satisfactory decision-making patterns

Honeymoon

1. Developing competence to participate in an intimate sexual relationship with the partner
2. Developing competence to live in close association with the partner

1. Developing a basis for mutually satisfactory sexual relationship

2. Developing a mutually satisfactory shared experience as a basis for later relationship of husband and wife

Early marriage

1. Taking part in establishing a home base

2. Accommodating daily living patterns to the situation of being married
3. Developing further sexual adequacy

1. Working with spouse to set up home base, developing appropriate skills

2. Developing a mutual satisfying network of external relations
3. Further developing an internal family organization for managing the routine of family life

71

Early Marriage

4. Developing appropriate commitment to the marital relationship
5. Developing a self-conception congruent with the role conception

Interpersonal

4. Developing positive orientation to the marriage and mutual esteem

Social influences

Mary Richmond was of the opinion that the social worker or, as she significantly termed him, 'the Social Adjuster', could not succeed in America 'without sympathetic understanding of the Old World backgrounds from which his clients came'.[25] This statement has compelling force today, when in this country we attempt to help people recently who had immigrated to this country from cultures with which we have very little knowledge. Yet it is not, of course, only immigrants who 'have backgrounds'.

One aspect of background with which social workers have always had to deal, but now more than ever, is that aspect covered by the term 'class'. This is a term which apparently is somewhat emotive, and social workers often object to considering people as belonging to a particular social class. Yet observers have often drawn our attention to the ways in which ideas, style of life, opportunities and other aspects of behaviour are significantly related to one's position in the class structure. Thus Masterman, early in the present century, suggested that most failures in legislation and social experiment were due to neglect of the fact of social class difference:

It has **been assumed** that the artisan is but a stunted or distorted specimen of the small tradesman: with the same ideals, the same aspirations, the same limitations; demanding the same moulding towards the fashioning of a completed product. We are gradually learning that 'the people of England' are as different from, and as unknown to, the classes that investigate, observe and record, as the people of China or Peru . . . these people grow and flourish and die, with their own code of honour, their special beliefs and moralities, their judgement and often their condemnation of the classes to whom has been given leisure and material advantage.[26]

This, of course, refers to an earlier time than the present, and it might be argued that social conditions have now changed to such an extent that it paints a false picture. It could be argued that there is now very much more harmony and much more common purpose between the social classes. It is important for the social worker to consider the evidence for and against this.

There is, for example, a considerable amount of evidence for the existence of class differences in important aspects of child rearing. Kohn found in America that middle-class parents tended to rear their children in a way which would establish within the child an internal standard of behaviour, whilst working-class parents trained their children so that they would fear to violate certain prescriptions in relation to their behaviour.[27] In Britain considerable attention is being paid to the place of language in child-rearing, and the work of Bernstein in the late 1950s has already been the subject of lengthy critical analysis.[28] The exact relationship between the structure of our society and our language and learning is not yet clear, but the topic is clearly one of the greatest importance for social workers, partly because they rely themselves so heavily upon language. An example of the kind of finding which the theorists are trying to illuminate can be taken from a recent study of child-rearing practices in Nottingham.[29] It was found that mothers at the upper end of the social class scale relied heavily on the use of reasoned verbal explanation in the attempt to make their children behave acceptably; those at the lower end of the scale were much less concerned with verbal communication of any sort. It appears that there is a social class difference in the valuation placed upon words as agents of truth:

For the professional-class mother, the putting of an idea into words invests it with a permanence which cannot be ignored; she will therefore take great care not to say anything to the child which might be considered un-

73

truthful. . . . As one descends the social scale, however, the general attitude towards what it is, or is not, permissible to say to the child becomes far more a matter of convenience and quick results. If the truth cannot (in the mother's opinion) be told, as in the case of sex questions, then 'making up some little fairy story' is considered a perfectly feasible alternative by almost half of all (in sample) working-class mothers. . . .

This finding illustrates the existence of class differences in the practice of child rearing, but social class influences should not be treated as if they were crucial only at the beginning of life, as it were. We are coming to appreciate that socialization (training for social roles) occurs throughout life and that there are many points of role-change where new learning or re-learning is important. To take a small, but relevant example: people may at certain points in their lives seek social work help. In this situation they have to learn a new role, that of client; they have to learn appropriate feeling and behaviour. It is at such a learning point that social class factors may be important. Studies in America, for example, suggest that the kind of psychiatric treatment given to the mentally ill is highly influenced by social class factors.[30] Similar factors may account for the very high proportion of social work clients who do not continue contact with the agency.

KNOWLEDGE OF THE SOCIAL SERVICES

Services designed to help people in different kinds of difficulty have been evolving quite rapidly in the present decade or so, and the consequent complex agencies, personnel and eligibility rules seems often to constitute a considerable barrier between the social worker and the potential client. Some commentators are so impressed with the complexity of the world of welfare that they see the primary function of the social worker as to act as a kind of signpost to the appropriate service. This is clearly an important task, but more is involved than the provision of directions. The process of referral to a social agency or from one social agency to another is worthy of further investigation, but at present it seems to involve a number of different aspects. These will begin to become apparent as we see how the process is seen in the following account of referral from the client of a social work agency:

I had been visited by Miss L. for about six months. One day I sensed that something was the matter. Miss L. said that she had been thinking about the way things had been going and she thought that I was now managing quite well. I said that I thought things were better, but I was still worried about Michael (her eldest son). Miss L. said, yes, she thought I would be and she wondered if I would agree to seeing someone at the hospital about him. She knew a Miss – I forget her name, but she did say a name to me. I thought to myself that I did not want Miss L. to go, and then I became suddenly worried about Michael. Miss L. had been coming from the Welfare, but now she thought that I should go to the hospital. I worried that she must think he was very much worse and that there was nothing more she could do for him or for that matter, for me. Miss L. seemed to know something was up with me. She said she would be sorry to stop coming, but that I was doing so much better with the budgeting and all that. She would leave it with me to think over for a week or so and call again to see what I thought.

In this extract it appears that the social worker considers that the client could more appropriately be helped by being transferred to the medical social worker at the hospital (which Michael was attending in connection with his asthma). It might well appear sensible that now the client was coping better with one set of problems (budgeting) she should be transferred to another social worker, who would concentrate on a different aspect (for example, her feelings in relation to Michael's complaint). Yet to the client it is the possible significance of the referral that seems crucial: does it mean that the situation is now considered so serious that more intensive 'medical' intervention is necessary? In other situations the client may experience referral or the talk of referral as rejection on the part of the original worker or as a clear sign that her condition or her family's is beyond help or remedy. If, then, we see referral as a process it implies that the social worker should know not only which services are appropriate in a general way, but also their possible significance for members of our society.

The caseworker in the extract we are discussing was able to name a particular person in the hospital medical social work department, and this sign of knowledge of what she was referring the client to might well be taken by the client as an indication of interest. Knowledge of other agencies is an important ingredient in the social worker's intellectual equipment and it takes two forms. First, general knowledge of provision available, and of the way in which it is offered. Thus, it is important to know not simply the various kinds of help available, say to the aged, but also the problems in such services, the way the personnel are likely to react and so on. Second, the social worker should develop particular knowledge of the provision within his (or her) own area, so that the doubts, anxieties and lack of knowledge of people seeking help other than that which he can provide, can be dealt with as precisely as possible.

But knowledge of other services often concerns rights as much as information about what is or is not available. This involves the social worker in a more active role than many seem inclined to adopt, but as Brooke has recently pointed out: 'Not only do they [people] need information, but the more inarticulate and timid clients of the social services need spokesmen, negotiators and sometimes advocates.'[31] An example of advocacy has recently been described in the case of a problem family.[32] The father of a family of seven children (six at home) applied to the local office of the Supplementary Benefits Commission for a grant towards the cost of clothing the children. He had been unemployed for many years. The original application was refused and the man decided to appeal:

But he had every reason for doubt as to the possibility of

success. He does not possess the qualities and abilities necessary to reasonable presentation of his 'case'. He is unable to express himself adequately in speech and his reaction to the frustration this arouses is sometimes a violent one – a characteristic which has not (and understandably) endeared him to the many officials of government with whom, he has, over the years, been in a state of almost constant conflict.

In this situation two members of the local authority, one of whom was a trained social worker, decided to appear as the man's representatives before the Appeals Tribunal. The hearing went in the man's favour and the tribunal awarded the sum of £25 for clothing. His response was of interest, '*You* won there – not me! They will listen to university people – but not to the likes of us', to which the authors add, 'And who – in knowledge of the fruitless attempts he has made on his own behalf to secure some recognition of the reality of his material needs – could deny this?'

KNOWLEDGE IN APPLICATION

So far we have been considering knowledge in a general manner, and often in a way that indicated the considerable deficiencies in our present ability to control and to predict behaviour. Yet the social worker has to use what general knowledge is available in the attempt to help a particular individual or group of individuals to solve specific problems. In the first chapter we discussed the case of Mary, a young unmarried girl expecting a baby. If we now indicate the theoretical knowledge available to help the social worker to deal with this particular problem we shall perhaps begin to see some of the problems which arise in the application of knowledge.

It is possible to see three kinds of knowledge as relevant to this particular problem: general ideas about the social problem of which this is an instance; theories of causation; and the experience of social workers, particularly in relation to the girl's decision about the baby's future.

The social problem of the unmarried mother

In dealing with the case of Mary, the social worker will have in mind some ideas concerning the size of the problem and the sort of problem it is, so that some assessment can be made of the typicality of Mary's situation.

During the last decade or so the number of illegitimate births in England and Wales has more than doubled: in 1955 there were nearly 31,500 such births or 4·6 of all live births; in 1965 the corresponding figures were 66,780 or 7·8 per cent. The illegitimacy ratio (the number of illegitimate births per 100 live births) has risen very sharply. There have in fact been only two similar increases in the last 100 years, and these were both associated with the very disturbed social conditions of the world wars. This helps to give the general problem some perspective, but we have to recognize that in this, as in other areas, the statistics conceal important dimensions of the problem. The counting of illegitimate births, like the counting of criminals, the mentally ill and so on, often groups together those who should be separately identified. It is difficult, for example, in the statistics we are discussing to know how many illegitimate births 'belong' to single women, and how many to cohabiting couples; or the proportion of second and subsequent births. These are important facts that are missing from our present picture, but the available statistics are of considerable help at least in so far as they help to correct our imaginary view of the extent and nature of the problem.

Many people when they think of a social problem (say crime or mental illness) readily entertain in their minds a picture of what is apparently the typical instance. There seems to be available, as it were, in any society a stereotype of the typical madman, criminal and so on. In Victorian society, for example, the picture of 'the fallen woman' probably played some part in the processes by which women were recruited to this particular role. In the case of the unmarried mother today we perhaps think of the 'typical' case as that of a teenager, rebelling against parental moral rules, and basically out for a good time. The statistics help us to correct such a view, at least in one important respect. The Registrar General has pointed out that although the probability of having an illegitimate child is high for the teenage girl (because more than half of the unmarried women of child bearing age are in this category), the probability that an unmarried woman will conceive in the course of a year is higher for those aged 20-24 and 25-29.[33] A study of illegitimate maternities in Scotland indicated that nearly a third of illegitimate births were to girls who were not single (i.e., married, widowed or divorced).[34]

But what are the characteristics of the situation that constitute a social problem. Can the social worker's concern for Mary be justified on social grounds? This obviously entails some sort of definition of a social problem. If we accept as a reasonable working definition that a social problem is a repetitive series of situations (comprising human behaviour and exigencies) which are experienced as a threat to existing social institutions and beliefs, it is clear that a case could be made for judging that the unmarried mother constitutes a social problem in any of the three phases through which she has passed. By the three phases I refer to sexual intercourse outside marriage, pregnancy and the birth of an illegitimate child.

It is of some importance to distinguish between the three phases which together constitute the problem condition, especially since explanations of the problem seem, until recently, to have assumed that the same theory would necessarily cover all the phases together. We can assume a relatively large population of unmarried women who have intercourse outside marriage, a smaller population who become pregnant, and a still smaller population that carries the child to term. At each stage there is, as it were, a shrinkage of population, and we need to know why some start the journey at all, and why they arrive at the second and third points of departure. This aspect of the problem will be discussed later when we consider explanatory theories, but at this stage we should perhaps note that there may well be disagreement about the extent to which each phase itself constitutes a social problem.

This is most likely to arise in connection with the first phase. All societies seek to control sexual activity in a variety of ways, but many of them make some distinction between couples who can and those who cannot legitimately engage in sexual intercourse outside marriage. Thus, a study of 67 different societies found that sexual intercourse between a couple who were betrothed was punished in only 10 per cent of the societies.[35] In our own society it seems clear that sexual relations outside marriage between socially unrelated people is by no means unusual, though it is difficult to say if it is becoming more common. Two points arise from this. First, the fact that such relations are known to be common weakens that aspect of social control which relied on perpetuating the idea that 'only certain kinds of (not very nice) girls engaged in that kind of thing'. Second, social attitudes seem to point in two different directions at least with regard to this issue. On the one hand, sexual titillation appears to be openly encouraged by means of advertisement and mass communications media. On the other, social norms forbidding sexual relations outside marriage are still widely upheld, and little help is available to those 'foolish' enough to become pregnant.

So far, we have been implicitly assuming a particular definition of the problem: we have been concentrating attention on the unmarried *mother*. This, of course, is to define the father completely out of the picture. It is remarkable how in practice, and theory also, he is often completely excluded. Some of the main theories that claim to account for the illegitimate child born to the young unmarried person focus exclusively upon the woman, stressing, for example, the disturbance of her emotional relationships with one or both of her parents. If we examine the kinds of help available we see that these often exclude the father from contact with the child or from participating in planning for its future. This exclusion could be seen simply as a product of the double standard that still exists in relation to sexual morality; a higher standard of behaviour is expected from the women. It is possible, however, that it has a more interesting significance, which might be important for those wanting to understand the complex relationships that exist between a problem and the service 'designed' to solve it. Fathers may be excluded because the institution of marriage and the family might appear to be threatened if the social services concerned did anything that might be counted as recognizing the unmarried couple and their child as a viable social unit. Hence the emphasis on the mother and child. The institution of marriage is further safeguarded if we are able to label the unmarried father as 'seducer' and 'ne'er-do-well', since this suggests that the girl did not 'choose' to enter into a sexual liaison with him: had she not been 'forced' or 'misled' she would undoubtedly have staunchly upheld the virtues of unmarried sexual continence. In addition the fact that she was in some way not responsible for what happened (the father is so responsible) means that it is socially possible to help her, even though she has transgressed important, if uncertain, sexual rules.

Theories of causation

If we try to understand the causation of illegitimacy, which, as we have seen, is different from understanding either sexual intercourse outside marriage or pregnancy resulting from this, it seems that there are two main theoretical approaches, the cultural and the psychological. These two approaches have been elaborated most extensively in America, where it seems to be broadly true that illegitimacy in the negro is explained in cultural terms, whilst the privileged White American is apparently entitled to a psychoanalytic explanation.

Illegitimacy amongst the American negroes, is explained on the basis that sexual misconduct is culturally more acceptable amongst the non-white population. This more accepting behaviour is explained, in its turn, by historical reasons. Secure family life has seldom been possible for the American negro, either because of the conditions of slavery or because, in more recent times, negroes have been moving from the South to the urban and industrialized north. At first sight this interpretation seems plausible, but there is conflicting evidence. For example, it seems that in Jamaica women who bear children within an unrecognized 'marriage' or as a result of casual relationships do in fact suffer some social disability.[36] An American study in 1960 of more than 600 negro mothers whose youngest child was illegitimate concluded: 'All but a few felt great guilt at having illegitimate children . . . these mothers did not accept illegitimacy as a normal way of life. They resented their status and recognized the handicaps.'[37] These findings cannot, of course, be taken to rule out any explanation of illegitimacy that centres on differential norms. Social workers need to keep constantly in mind the idea that behaviour which may be in some way reprehensible to them may be normal or even praiseworthy to others. At the same time the conflicting evidence in regard to the influence of different norms in the case of negro illegitimacy provides a necessary reminder of the difficulty of becoming sure that the differences are more real than apparent.

The other main approach to the causation of the illegitimate birth is to be found in psychoanalytic theory. The kind of interpretation this yields can be found in the following excerpt:

> When discussing unmarried mothers we are talking of a very special group of girls who have not only 'got into trouble' but who have failed to adopt any of the alternatives (savoury or unsavoury) to unmarried motherhood. A girl in our society who starts a pregnancy with a man whom she is either unwilling or unable to marry, has shown herself to be a disturbed personality, and I think we are entitled to look upon an illegitimate baby as the living proof of his mother's severe emotional difficulties.[38]

There are, of course, various ideas about the nature of the girl's emotional disturbance. Some would stress the psychological character of the girl, so that she was seen as essentially narcissistic or self-regarding. Others would see the source of her disturbance in faulty relationships from an early age with mother or with father. Yet others would argue that the girl was caught up in a tempestuous relationship between the parents. Yet whatever the form of the disturbance, an approach based upon the primary importance of long-standing emotional disturbance must answer the persistent question: how does the theory square with the empirical evidence?

The empirical evidence is, as is often the case in issues concerning the social worker, inconclusive. In America, Vincent's study concluded that 'Unwed motherhood is not the result of any one personality type, intrafamilial relationship or social situation'.[39] The study of illegitimate maternities in Scotland already referred to suggests, however, that illegitimacy is not spread evenly throughout the population: 'It is evident that illegitimacy tends to be associated with unskilled, unattractive, or menial occupations.' Evidence from other sources suggests that this concentration cannot be explained by any drop in the status of occupation following knowledge of the conception.

Experiences of social workers

If we examine the knowledge so far reviewed it will be evident that it provides no overwhelming indication for a social worker wanting to know how to help an unmarried mother; we see instead only confusion about the kind of problem of which she is a part, and some interesting speculations about its causation. We know enough at least not to jump to conclusions, and to appreciate that in any given case either psychological or sociological factors may be predominant. Yet social workers have been trying to help the unmarried mother for many years, and during this time they have gained considerable experience about how to handle the problem. Admittedly there have been considerable changes of fashion. For the first two decades of this century, perhaps longer, the sole concern of the social work agency was the baby. None the less, over the years a volume of experience has been accumulated. The problem is, how can we utilize it?

If we examine the work undertaken with the unmarried

mother, it is clear that much of it revolves around the mother's decision regarding the future of the child: should she keep it, or place it for adoption or postpone a decision, making some kind of temporary arrangement for the care of the child in the meantime? Social workers have tried to help girls with this decision. What have they discovered about it?

One way to show economically the kind of experience social workers have had of this problem is to investigate recorded cases which have included the decision to part with or keep an illegitimate child. Thus, an American project[40] studied all unmarried mother cases in a social work agency over a period of time, and background data was obtained on such items as age, race, religion, education, employment history, financial status, family composition, residential history, and relation to the putative father. Those who surrendered their babies were compared with those who kept them. It was found possible to predict that the white girl was likely to surrender the baby if two or more of the following items were present in her background: she was a non-Catholic, had higher education, and was under eighteen, and the putative father was single. These indicating factors did not, of course, function in isolation and further analysis showed that the most important factors could be grouped together in terms of social class: 'Cases with a high loading in this factor, i.e. cases which are effectively described by the variables which make up this factor are characterized by coming from white, non-broken, middle or upper-class families, having held a white-collar or professional job, living in a shelter during pregnancy, having group therapy experience while in the shelter, and surrendering the baby.'

This is a method of summarizing social work experience with the decision unmarried mothers have to make about the future status of the child. It is a method that has been fruitfully applied to other important decisions in social service, e.g., the selection of foster parents. Two points should perhaps be made in connection with social work. First, empirical prediction cannot take the place of the judgment of the social worker, though it can help to inform and sharpen such judgment. Second, the factors tested are chosen because they are those that can be found recorded in most, if not all, cases. Broadening the basis for the selection of factors is dependent on detailed and systematic case recording, and on the development of categories that will help us to describe psychological as well as social background dimensions.

CONCLUSIONS

The social worker is faced with a bewildering and growing collection of facts, concepts, theories and speculations. The social worker has to try to use these so that his or her activity can claim to be informed. But a social worker cannot simply work on 'the facts' even if these were known. Some work of interpretation is always required. The kind of work this might be can be well illustrated from a recent discussion by Wilson of 'the facts about the sexual behaviour of the young'.[41] Wilson uses for this discussion Schofield's survey, *The Sexual Behaviour of Young People*. In this work sexual activities are divided into types: dating, kissing, deep kissing, etc., up to sexual intercourse. This seems a satisfactory procedure and produces interesting results, but, as Wilson argues,

> . . . it would be premature to assume that we can use the results of his survey to talk generally about 'the sexual behaviour' of young people. This is not because the survey is in any way misconceived as a piece of sociological research: it is rather because of the gap between his operational definition of 'sexual behaviour' . . . and the general meaning of such terms. . . . How do we know that the 'dating' category is always a *sexual* category? What do we mean by 'sexual activity' anyway? These are questions which we must answer if we are to say anything in *our normal language* about 'sexual' behaviour, *or if we are going to apply research results to some form of practical action*. . . .

NOTES

[1] For instance, 'Students (of social work) need more knowledge of the family as a social unit. . . . They need more skill in securing adequate understanding of group members' familial situations. They need increased ability to use that understanding. . . . 'Students need more understanding of the family as a reference group. . . .' Murphy, M., *The Social Group Work Method in Social Work Education*, New York: Council on Social Work Education, 1959, pp. 16-17.

[2] Loch, C. S., 'An A.B.C. for Almoners', *Charity Organization Society Review*, October 1897.

[3] *Annual Report* of the Charity Organization Society, 1933/4.

[4] Goetschius, G., *Working with Unattached Youth*, London: Routledge & Kegan Paul, 1967, p. 142.

[5] Buzelle, G., 'Individuality in the Work of Charity', Proceedings of the 13th National Conference of Charities and Correction, (U.S.A.), 1886.

[6] Bosanquet, S. R., *The Rights of the Poor and Christian Almsgiving Vindicated*, p. 77.

[7] Rall, M., 'The effective use of Case-Work Principles in the Family Agency', *Social Service Review*, September 1950.

[8] Eliot, T. D., 'Sociology as a Pre-vocational Subject: the Verdict of Sixty Social Workers', *American Journal of Sociology*, XXIX, May 1924.

[9] ibid.

[10] *Report* of the (Seebohm) Committee on Local Authority and Allied Personal Social Services, Cmnd.3703, S.455, 1968.

[11] Emerson, R., 'On Gifts', in his *Essays*, Chicago: Spencer Press, 1936.

[12] Saint Augustine, *Confessions*, Book II, Chapter 6, pp. 49-50, London: Penguin.

[13] Reynolds, B., *Social Work and Social Living*, New York: Citadel Press, 1951.

[14] Milford Conference, 'Generic and Specific', *A Report of the American Association of Social Workers*, New York: Dominican Association of Social Workers, 1929.

[15] Karpf, J., *The Scientific Basis of Social Work*, New York: Columbia University Press, p. 90.

[16] Richmond, M., *Social Diagnosis*, New York: Russell Sage Foundation, 1917, p. 376.

[17] Mills, C. W., *The Sociological Imagination*, London: Oxford University Press, 1959, p. 161.

[18] Jefferys, M., *An Anatomy of Social Welfare Services*, London: Michael Joseph, 1965.

[19] Study of Rothbart and Macoby quoted in Dornbusch, S., 'Afterword' in the *Developments of Sex Differences*, ed. S. Maccoby, London: Tavistock, 1967.

[20] Hartley, R., 'Children's concepts of male and female roles', quoted by Dornbusch, op. cit.

[21] Dearden, R., 'The Aims of Primary Education', in *Perspectives on Plowden*, ed. Peters, R., London: Routledge & Kegan Paul, 1969.

[22] Jehu, D., 'A Scientific Psychological Approach in the Teaching of Human Growth and Behaviour', *Case Conference*, June 1967.

[23] Rayner, E., 'Elementary Education in Human Developments', *Case Conference*, May 1967.

[24] Rapoport, R., 'The Study of Marriage as a Critical Transition for Personal and Family Development' in *The Predicament of the Family*, ed. Lomas, P., London: Hogarth Press, 1967.

[25] Richmond, M., *What is Social Case Work?*, New York: Russell Sage Foundation, 1922, p. 118.

[26] Masterman, C. F., *The Condition of England*, London: Methuen, 1909, pp. 111-12.

[27] Kohn, M., 'Social Class and the Exercise of Parental Authority', *American Sociological Review*, XXIV, 1959.

[28] See Lawton, D., *Social Class, Language and Education*, London: Routledge & Kegan Paul, 1968.

[29] Newson, J. and Newson, E., 'Some Social Differences on the Process of Child Rearing', *Penguin Social Sciences Survey 1968*, ed. J. Gould.

[30] See e.g. Grill, N. and Storrow, H., 'Social Class and Psychiatric Treatment', *Mental Health of the Poor*, ed. Riessman, F., et al, New York: Free Press of Glencoe, 1964.

[31] Brooke, R., 'Civic Rights and Social Services', *Political Quarterly*, vol. 40. No. 1., January-March, 1969.

[32] Haywood, S. and Fox, W., 'Administrative Justice?', *Case Conference*, March 1968.

[33] General Register Office, *Report of Registrar General* (England and Wales) 1964.

[34] Thompson, B., 'Social Study of Illegitimate Maternities', *British Journal of Preventive and Social Medicine*, X, 1956.

[35] Brown, J. S., 'A Comparative Study of Deviation from Sexual Mores', *American Sociological Review*, April 1952.

[36] Blake, J., *Family Structure in Jamaica*, Free Press of Glencoe, 1961

[37] Greenleigh Associates, *Facts, Fallacies and Future, A study of the Aid to Dependent's Children, Programme of Cook County, Illinois, 1960*, New York, 1960.

[38] Gough, D., 'Work with Unmarried Mothers', *The Almoner*, March 1961.

[39] Vincent, C., *Unmarried Mothers*, Free Press of Glencoe, 1961.

[40] Meyer, H., Jones W. and Borgatta, E., 'The Decision by Unmarried Mothers to Keep or Surrender their Babies', *Social Work* (U.S.), April 1956.

[41] Wilson, J., Williams N., and Sugarman, B., *Introduction to Moral Education*, London: Penguin, 1967.

4

The Methods of Social Work

THIS CHAPTER WILL be concerned with certain aspects of what are usually described as the three methods of social work – social casework, social groupwork and community work. There are very many questions that could be asked about the status and content of these methods, but this chapter will discuss each of the methods in a highly selective way. The aim will be to raise issues that are of general importance to social work even though the discussion of each selected issue will be rooted in one particular method. In the consideration of social casework we shall be concerned largely with historical and contemporary criticism of the method; in the section on groupwork we shall raise mainly technical questions, whilst the comments on community work will seek to understand the identity of this comparatively new method of work. Clearly, critical appraisal, technical development, and identity are not issues that can be restricted to any one method, and equally clearly they are collectively important for the development of social work.

Before we discuss methods in more detail, however, it is important to appreciate that such terms as 'method' belong to a family of terms (including also such frequently used concepts as 'technique' and 'skill') which refer broadly to the technical aspects of social work. Such terms are usually unstable; that is, they are often used interchangeably to refer sometimes to what appear to be the same and sometimes different phenomena. Some writers refer to the three main subdivisions as 'methods', whilst others talk of the methods of one such division (e.g., the methods of social casework). Sometimes a technique is mistaken for 'a scientific approach' or for 'skill'. Thus, the Annual Report of the C.O.S. 1934/5 speaks of the importance of a student acquiring 'a technique of interviewing, a technique in obtaining information, a technique in listening'. There is nothing to be gained from the attempt to freeze particular meanings onto these terms so that they may enjoy an eternally fixed identity, but a discussion involving them does need to start with a fairly clear idea about the meaning of the terms. Some practitioners or some of those concerned with the practical nature of social work may object that this preliminary has little consequence for the 'real' world, and that it is simply an academic exercise. To argue in this way, however, is to suggest either that we can without loss dispense with concepts like 'skill', 'method', and so on, or that we already know how to use them well enough. Neither of these positions can be accepted.

Consequently, in discussing social work methods, some kind of differentiation should be made between the main terms. A 'method' could, for instance, be said to be a stabilized collection or grouping of techniques and its associated focus of knowledge. Thus 'method' would be restricted to the methods of social work, i.e., casework, groupwork and community work. These methods are informed by ideas, theories and factual descriptions that can be said to provide a focus. A social worker's basic knowledge may contain many elements required for the practice of social work according to any method, but none the less it appears sensible to think that as the social worker's attention moves from the individual in his family to the larger group system, and then to the relations between large groups and the wider society, there is some change in the focus of knowledge. 'Technique', on the other hand, could be used to refer to a standardized way of achieving a particular objective. Thus, within community work method it would be possible to refer to different techniques of community analysis, or within groupwork to different techniques of intervention within a group. 'Skill' is perhaps best used simply as a habit of using the technique well; it refers to dexterity in actual performance.

SOCIAL CASEWORK

This method is the most well established, and has the most extensive supporting literature. The term was used originally in a non-technical sense to refer simply to the method of working 'case by case' as opposed to the attempt to solve people's problems by any general solution. It is in this sense that people other than social workers still refer to their casework; for instance, the Parliamentary Commissioner works with individual situations of possible maladministration – he does casework. In social work, however, the term came quite quickly to express much more clearly certain value aspects and to stand for individualism in a way that seemed to suggest no generalization was proper, and that the only cure for a wide range of social problems was on the basis of an individual relationship between client and caseworker.

Early critics of social casework, at least as it was practised by the Charity Organization Society, praised certain aspects of its methodology, whilst condemning both the attitudes of the workers and the social philosophy from which they seemed naturally to arise. Some of the attitudes can be seen in the following quotation from an article published as late as 1924:

> To put aside conventions and the distinctions of class is not so hard. Even to refuse to be shocked at the confession of sins we have no mind to, and to realize our common heritage of sin is possible enough. . . . but the effort to realize our common brotherhood with a man of weak and shifting character is an effort indeed, which only charity can make effective. . . . To have sympathy is good, but to show it too eagerly is sometimes not good. A smack of the orderly room is more to the point. . . .[1]

It is easy to see in attitudes such as these, evidence for Beatrice Webb's judgment that the Charity Organization Society, 'had not the faintest glimmer of what I have called "the consciousness of collective sin" '[2] and that its workers entertain a 'calm assumption of social superiority over the poor whom they visited'.[3] Yet we would miss some of the subtlety of the situation if we did not recognize that any claim to 'unshockability' *is* facile if it concerns only 'sins we have no mind to', and that each period in history presents a particular social type or types which contemporaries cannot accept into 'the common brotherhood' without difficulty. Today we may not find 'the weak and shifting' type so difficult to accept, but this does not mean that we can easily act as if we were at one with all types and conditions of men or that we can so act at all, unless charity makes our work effective.

A similar kind of balanced appraisal also needs to be employed when we consider the more important criticisms that the early caseworkers were technically pure, but philosophically tainted. Beatrice Webb, for example, was able to praise the casework of the C.O.S. on three grounds: it assumed 'patient and persistent personal service on the part of the well-to-do'; it was based upon 'an acceptance of personal responsibility for the ulterior consequences, alike to the individual recipient and to others who might be indirectly affected, of charitable assistance'; it was a realization of 'the application of the scientific method to each separate case . . . so that the assistance given should be based on a correct forecast of what would actually happen, as a result of the gift, to the character and circumstances of the individual recipient and to the destitute to which he belonged'.[4] These three principles Beatrice Webb found acceptable, even praiseworthy, but she could only condemn the theorizing of those caseworkers who restricted their charity to the 'deserving' poor and the leading members of the C.O.S. who 'added to their sectarian creed as to the necessary restrictions of the impulse of charity, an equally determined resistance to any extension of State or municipal action. . . . whilst advocating, in occasional asides, or by parenthetical phrases, the moralization of the existing governing class'.[5]

Again such criticisms seem plausible, but if we simply take Beatrice Webb's words as they stand we may miss an opportunity of extending our understanding of the development of social casework. For example, Beatrice Webb praised the pursuit of 'the scientific method' in social casework. Laying aside the question already raised in Chapter 3 concerning the extent to which it is possible to describe social work in any of its methods as 'scientific', it is worthwhile enquiring a little more closely into the early caseworker's quest for knowledge – it was more interestingly ambivalent than Beatrice Webb leads us to imagine. On the one hand, caseworkers were encouraged to develop their knowledge not only of the individual client, but also of the district in which they worked:

> Nothing but an intimate knowledge of the conditions under which our poor neighbours live, can give us true sympathy with their lives and enable us to divine where their real difficulties lie; and one, if not the only, way of getting this knowledge and wide sympathy is to set ourselves to a careful study of the district in which we desire to work – a study not only of the people themselves, but also of local institutions and customs which do so much to make the people what they are, and to which it is due that a district can be worked, not as a chaotic agglomeration of atoms, but as an organic whole.[6]

This quotation, which suggests also that early caseworkers did not focus as narrowly on the individual as their later more clinical successors, must be set alongside another extract from the same book, which suggests that the search for knowledge was often abruptly truncated and certainly would not have been allowed to lead to conclusions questioning basic assumptions of method: '. . . The great majority of cases fall into fairly well defined classes, and though the "treatment" must be modified in each particular case, yet it will run on more or less familiar lines'.[7]

But, as we have seen in Chapter 1, it is fairly easy to establish some important differences between the casework of the early decades of the present century and the method employed by the contemporary social worker. Some general picture of current social casework can be obtained from the following description:

> Casework is a personal service provided by qualified workers for individuals who require skilled assistance in resolving some material, emotional or character problem. It is a disciplined activity which requires a full appreciation of the needs of the client in his family and community setting. The caseworker seeks to perform this service on the basis of mutual trust and in such a way as will strengthen the client's own capacities to deal with problems and to achieve a better adjustment with his environment. The services required of a caseworker cover many kinds of human need, ranging from relatively simple problems of material assistance to complex personal situations involving serious emotional disturbance or character defect, which may require prolonged assistance and the careful mobilization of resources and of different professional skills.[8]

Examples of casework have already been given earlier in the book, and so at this stage it is appropriate to examine some of the more general questions raised by this description. We shall then turn to a discussion of problems in the current valuation of social casework as a social work method.

In the above quotation casework is described as a personal service, a disciplined activity, and so on, but such descriptions also apply to the work of other professionals, like doctors, priests and psychotherapists. At the same time it is correctly stated that caseworkers are called upon to deal with a very wide range of problems, so that it is not easy to distinguish casework in terms of its concern with particular difficulties. How, then, can we grasp the nature of social casework more surely? There is no immediate answer to this question, but we begin to discern the way if we bear in mind at least two observations. First, the exploration of the nature of social casework has often been needlessly complicated by the assumption that the objective was the discovery of an entity (a collection of knowledge and techniques) that was in every major respect unique. But, as the chapter on social work knowledge indicated, the knowledge on which social caseworkers might be said to rely, is in no way private or exclusive to casework, and the techniques of social casework (advice giving, reassurances and so on) have been part of social living for a long time. Second, whilst social caseworkers are concerned with problems of a material and emotional kind, the heart of their interest lies in the interaction between the material and the emotional, the personal and the social.

The objectives of social casework – or indeed of any social work method – have been stated frequently enough, but any formulation presents problems. In the quotation above, for example, the caseworker performs his service so that it 'will strengthen the client's own capacities to deal with his problems and to achieve a better adjustment with his environment'. Such a formulation seems to set the problem and its solution too firmly 'within' the individual, and pays too little attention to the logic of adjustment. Adjustment, as applied to relations between people, refers to a process whereby some balance is achieved between the states of the 'parties' concerned. When Mary Richmond referred to the social worker as a 'social adjuster' she was thinking very much in engineering terms; the social worker acted upon the other 'party'. In the light of this usage of the term it is probably more helpful to think of the caseworker as concerned with the adjustment between the client and his environment, since this recognizes that the solution to the client's problems is often to be found mainly, or in part in some change, more or less drastic, in his environment. This, however, does not remove all the difficulties associated with the formulation, since environment is such a global term ranging from a man's immediate family to the whole world as it impinges on him. As we consider the ever widening circles that encompass any man it is impossible to accept that adjustment between himself and any one circle will automatically produce adjustment in all the others. Thus, a man may reach an adjustment between his problems of masculinity and the demands of his wife, but this adjustment in his immediate environment may well produce difficulties in relations with his mother, his workmates, and so on.

The present crisis in social casework

Social casework is at present the object of considerable if rather diffuse adverse criticism. One well-known social worker teacher in America has considered it appropriate to consider critically the statement, 'Casework is Dead'.[9] What are the sources of current dissatisfaction?

Firstly, critics are re-emphasizing a question that has been present since the first formulations of social casework, namely, why spend time and energy dealing with casualties one by one, when a concerted attack on factors producing the problems would be more effective? It was this general argument that Beatrice Webb expressed when she questioned the value of rescuing people from the swamp rather than draining it. One possible reply to this is to suggest that whilst we know something about helping people one by one, we know very little about helping them by collective action. Such a point of view has been well expressed in the following passage from one of Iris Murdoch's novels:

> 'What's the use of preventing a man from stumbling when he's on a sinking ship?'
> 'Because if he breaks his ankle he won't be able to swim,' I suggested.
> 'But why try to save him from breaking his ankle if you can try to save him from losing his life?'
> 'Because I know how to do the former but not the latter,' I told him rather testily.'

> (*The Net*, p. 112)

In much the same tenor, Eleanor Rathbone once wrote to her friend Hilda Oakley:

> I like the despised C.O.S. work so much. If one's large

schemes fail, if dock labour is never properly organized, or the executive power better guided, or any question of philosophy elucidated, it will be a satisfaction at the end of life to know that, at any rate, some poor bicycle maker and his wife and children were set on their legs and saved from the House [the Work House] and made respectable citizens through my agency.[10]

Yet the claim that caseworkers know how to help people case by case could well be questioned. Such questioning constitutes the second source of current dissatisfaction with social casework, though again it is a matter of the greater emphasis on an attitude that has been present for some time. Currently the charge is made that social casework has retreated from the poor. This has not come about by deliberate design, though it has been suggested that the social worker's desire for social status would be furthered if it could be successfully claimed that a high proportion of her clients were middle class. Indeed, some of those anxious to protect 'the poor' would encourage the move towards thinking of social work as a way of helping, irrespective of the income or the social class of the person helped. The present criticism is that the very method of casework, the techniques employed, systematically deter groups of clients from making use of the services. There has in the past been sporadic recognition of the fact that parts of the procedure in social work agencies provoked a reaction or had unfortunate effects, but these reactions were interpreted within the framework of those offering the service rather than the recipients. Thus, it was recognized that part of the procedure of investigation could be resented by the applicant. Miss Lyons, for example, writing on the 'Art of Helping' in 1908 argued, 'We cannot find out the true cause of distress until we have made some enquiry'. She went on to ask:

What right have I to ask these questions. and to enquire into the private affairs of this man, who is almost a stranger to me, and who has the same right as I might have myself to resent this interference? The answer is

96

that we are supposing this family has asked for your help.
The man is not, therefore, a normal member of the
community. . . . it is unnatural, abnormal that he should
depend upon others. I am not saying that he is necessarily
to blame. Your child is not to blame for his sickness, yet
being sick he needs treatment such as would be quite
unsuitable to him in health.[11]

Here the argument is that the treatment, the medicine *is*
unpleasant, but necessary. At other times it was the repetition of certain procedures that was considered to have a
bad effect. Thus, the home visit was in order but 'a constant
intrusion into the houses of the poor, weakens their self-
respect'.[12] Again, it would be admitted that the procedures
were in themselves somewhat 'drastic', but that what made
them acceptable was the way in which the caseworker
administered them. For example, it was admitted to be
humiliating to be asked questions:

It *is* humiliating to be asked questions which imply
suspicion that one is a fraud; it is the most flattering thing
in the world to be asked exactly the same questions by
someone to whom the information seems to be interesting
and worth having. To achieve this latter technique, to
give psychological 'security' to the applicant – a security
which money cannot buy and only tact and understanding
can give – has been the main object of the C.O.S.
movement.[13]

It is not clear how far the humiliation is in any way
different from the flattery. Both attitudes are based on the
assumption that what is crucial is the perspective of the
social worker and what has to be achieved are his aims.

So, some reflection on the impact of casework can be
found in the past, but the current criticism is more
systematic and vigorous. It can be summed up perhaps by
using some words from the title of an article in the U.S.A. –
a disengagement from the poor. The retreat from the
culturally deprived has taken the form of failure to
appreciate that the methods employed in casework agencies

systematically ensure that some people get no help or an inferior kind of help or that they are deterred from applying because of the 'image' of the social work agency. As Reynolds said some years ago, social casework methods have become so refined that only the refined will use them.

The third source of discontent in connection with social casework arises from the sense that casework may not simply be failing 'the poor', but may simply be failing. As the demand for social workers increases and as expectations are heightened, the uneasiness grows that perhaps social casework cannot produce the goods or that the goods it tends to produce are not what we think they are or should be. The evaluation of social casework can encompass a range of objectives. Concern for efficiency is not a new phenomenon: 'We only want subscribers to care as much for the efficiency of a benevolent institution as shareholders do for that of a joint-stock company; and in general, that social work should be managed as intelligently as business or industry.'[14] Yet to ask that social work be efficient in the same way that industry is efficient is to focus on the end-product and to take attention away from what happens during the 'process of production', and this may well be the most important effect of the exercise. Yet efficiency cannot be assessed without some idea both of what is being assessed and of the purposes which it is supposed to achieve. Both these requirements pose very serious problems in social casework.

GROUP WORK

In this country social groupwork can encompass a range of activities from the organization of leisure programmes in a youth club to the kind of work illustrated in Chapter 2 which some would want to describe as psychotherapy. Similarly, those working with groups think of themselves as social workers or as part of the education service. In this section the emphasis will be placed on groupwork as a method of social work designed to help particular groups of clients to solve some problems they have in common. As such it is a method that is increasingly advocated, and social workers have now gained experience in conducting groups for adoptive parents, adolescents, foster parents (as we saw in Chapter 2), mothers of children attending child guidance clinics, girls in probation hostels, boys on probation, and so on. Groups, like individual interviews, can be used for a number of different purposes, but in this section we shall be concerned with elucidating the major technical questions facing a social worker who intends to use the groupwork method. In a simplified form these seem to be: whom to work with, what to work on and how to work.

Before discussing these questions, however, it is worth pausing to note some aspects of the claim that groupwork is a method of social work. That it is a *method* should become clear as the technical questions are discussed, but what makes it a social work method, and what is implied in the assertion of this character? Such questions are important for a consideration of the methods of social work whether collectively or one by one.

One answer is to suggest that groupwork is a method of social work because it has the same value basis as casework and community work. Thus, a social worker with previous experience of social casework has written, 'I have come to understand a little more what the right to self-determination may mean since I worked with groups'.[15] We shall see in Chapter 5 that the opportunity for such an increase in understanding should not be neglected, and the author continues by reinterpreting the term and illustrating the way group experience can illuminate it:

This so-called right is really a statement about man's inter-dependence and inter-relationship and is a right bounded by similar rights in others. The important questions about this right always arise on the boundary between the self and the other, and this is exactly the area where a group is mainly at work. I found that very seldom did a session go by in the group for psychiatric out-patients which I conducted, without some questions being raised about sharing between members or caring for members. At times these arose very dramatically, as in the following example:

One very depressed man began to threaten to kill himself. The group seemed to be egging him on and agreeing with him, that he need consider no one but himself. His life was his own and he could decide to take it. I was frightened and helpless and fortunately kept silent because I did not know what to say, and finally one of the women burst out: 'You can't do it – if you do, you've made me responsible and why should I live with that?' Then she turned on me saying she had never wanted to be made responsible for other people and now she was and it was a wicked burden.

Others, however, see in the assertion that groupwork is a method of social work, a way of delimiting the kinds of technique used and of excluding those that could be said to be psychotherapeutic. Such an intention seems to echo earlier fears in relation to social casework, when individual psychotherapy seemed to be the object of avoidance. It would be unfortunate if those using the groupwork method had to undergo the same experience as social caseworkers and spend rather profitless time arguing that the groups conducted by social workers are, or are not, 'psychotherapeutic'. It would seem preferable to argue that both caseworkers and groupworkers employ a range of techniques and that the important question of the distinction between psychotherapy and social work should not be decided exclusively on grounds of differential technique. Caseworkers employ techniques ranging, in Hollis's terminology,[16] from 'reflectic discussion of the genetic development of response patterns or tendences' to 'suggestion and advice'. Similarly, groupworkers can employ a range of techniques of intervention, from using the group as a kind of audience for work with individuals to seeking to interpret only what appears to be happening in the life of the group: from helping members of a group to deal with various kinds of material, (e.g., 'artistic' material in a young children's play group or planning a programme of activity in a group for adolescents) to establishing 'artificial' conditions which encourage interaction within the group and interpreting the consequent tensions and the changing patterns of relationship.

Whom to work with?

This question seems to call for two decisions: defining the group in general and establishing criteria for the selection of particular members. Thus, a social worker might be concerned to work in a group with mothers of children coming to the clinic or with a local tenants' group, but the group cannot be formed until the social worker has decided on criteria for selecting particular members: for example, will mothers of children with particular complaints be chosen, and will account be taken of age, social class, and so on? This decision about membership is one of the most important made by the groupworker, but it is difficult to discover either from the literature or from the experience of social workers criteria that are unambiguous. Thus, groups of people with the same problem or with mixed problems have worked well. It is perhaps more important to consider what have been termed behavioural as opposed to demographic criteria; that is, in selecting a particular group we should attend to such factors as the likely behaviour of members towards one another, for example their position on a shyness- aggression continuum, rather than their occupation. It has recently been suggested that judgments in this area could be much more systematically exploited, so that selection is much more firmly grasped as one of the groupworker's most crucial techniques. Shalinsky has reported the attempt to use Schutz's theory of Fundamental Interpersonal Relations Orientations to form compatible and incompatible groups.[17] Clearly much more work needs to be done in this area of selection, but selection procedures and decisions are of decisive importance in the creation of different kinds of group experience, and hence in the outcome of groupwork.

The decision about group membership is not always, of

course, within the social worker's power. In working with neighbourhood groups, tenants' associations, youth groups and so on, the social worker is faced with groups that are to a large extent 'given'. None the less, reflection on criteria will enable the groupworker to bear in mind the possibility of suggesting the formation of sub-groups, as it were, for particular purposes and the limitations imposed upon the group's objectives by the personalities involved in the group.

What to work on?

The decision about group membership is closely connected with the decision on what to work on, especially since individuals before joining a group will expect some discussion of its methods and objectives. In deciding what should be the main object of the group's work, the groupworker will consider two questions, and they will both be questions about 'boundaries'. Group members will require some idea about what they will be trying to keep at the centre of their attention, and 'where' they will be working – 'where' referring not to the geographical location of their meeting, important though this is, but to the particular boundary on which they will work. This will become clear as the discussion proceeds.

An example from group counselling in social work will demonstrate the first kind of consideration – what to work on. It is taken from a project of group counselling with adoptive families, in which group guidance rather than group therapy was taken as the main objective: [18]

> In group therapy the goal is to alter and improve deep-seated personality problems and where appropriate to interpret unconscious motivation. The type of groups described in this paper had, however, quite a different goal. They aimed at clarification and modification of attitudes and at the better and more relaxed social functioning of these couples as adoptive parents. Some groups became irritated by the lack of guidance and advice from the leader, but when this was purposefully

not made available, they looked at each other's experience of adoption for guidance. This was clearly a more effective way of helping them to find out for themselves what was the way of handling any aspect of the adoption situation.

In these groups it was the attitudes of members that provided the main focus of work, but attitudes relevant to their functioning as adoptive couples. Moreover, the approach to these attitudes was to be indirect. Indeed it might seem that the approach was so indirect that it seemed to deny that any informational content was appropriate or required. In fact, however, specific guidance and information was given, but in three limited areas only:

First, information was given from research findings about how adopted children nearly always meet comments from other children before or about the age of nine, and this was related to the normal fantasies of the nine-year-old child. Secondly, information was also given about the attitudes of adopted adolescents, and finally, reassurance was given that much of the 'acting out' behaviour, the jealousies etc., which were described by the parents were appropriate to any child of that particular age or stage of development.

This decision to give information on certain topics is clearly part of the decision about what to work on in these particular groups.

In these groups for adoptive parents, one set of decisions on the part of the worker concerned the boundary between group counselling and group therapy – it was to be attitudes in relation to a particular role (that of adoptive parents) that was to be the main object of work, not 'deep-seated personality problems'. The worker also had to decide 'where' the work should mainly be centred. By this I mean that groups are involved with three main sets of relationships, those between parts or aspects of the individual, those between group members, and those between the group and its external environment, and it is extremely difficult to hold each of these in focus at the same time. A decision is required concerning which set of relationships will provide the main place of work. For example, a group of boys in a probation hostel could be encouraged to concentrate on the boundary between themselves and their environment, that is, other residents in the hostel, other groups, the staff, visiting social workers, and so on. Alternatively, they could focus upon relationships within the group; for example, the meaning for all of them of the absence of one member or the obvious reluctance of others to attend. Or the focus could be on the examination of the impact on each individual's self-image when the group engages in a period of very aggressive or very depressed behaviour. No rigid distinction can be maintained or held between these points of attention, but the social worker for his or her own sake, and for the sake of the group, should know which boundary system will provide the most work for the group.

How to work?

Again it will by now be obvious that this question has already been touched upon in the consideration of the others: the three questions are closely inter-connected. Yet this question has also its special character. In posing the question, how to work, the social groupworker is asking about the terminology in which his or her interventions in the group will be made, and this is basically a question about the theory or theories to be used in understanding group processes. There are many different theories about groups available. Thus, in the sociological field Homans has examined the themes of leadership and group control, arguing that the leader who emerges in the group is the member who most closely conforms to the norms of the group.[19] In the area of psychodynamics various theories have been proposed. Bion,[20] for example, has posited two aspects of a group, its 'rational' work aimed at achieving the acknowledged purposes of the group and its changing unconscious assumptions, those of fight/flight, pairing and dependency. It is possible to criticize these theories on various grounds. For example, Sherwood[22] has suggested that Bion may be mistaken in assuming that only one basic assumption can be active in any group at a particular time, and that he seems to suggest two different explanations for the direction group interaction takes. On the one hand, he appears to state that all group interactions are the result of inherent drives to establish groups to satisfy needs that are only capable of satisfaction through group experience, and, on the other hand, that group interactions are essentially adaptations acquired in the face of social pressures. Yet social work practitioners faced with the many sociological and psychological theories must use them to make what sense they can of the groups with which they work, and must ask whether the criticisms that can be, and are, made of the theories, are relevant to their practical concerns. Are there criteria which help the social worker in this situation? It is, I think, possible to simplify the problem if we think of the groupworker, at present, looking for two types of theory. The groupworker requires a way of summarizing the changing relationships between group members, and also some kind of explanatory framework ('this particular combination of relationships is happening because . . .'). The first requirement can most easily be met through some kind of role inventory, some set of ideas about the main roles characteristically carried on in groups. In this connection the categories offered by Benne and Sheats[22] appear very useful. They differentiate between group-building roles (the member shows solidarity, tension release, or agrees), individual roles (shows antagonism, shows tension, disagrees), and group task roles (gives suggestions, gives opinions, gives orientations, asks suggestions, asks opinion, asks for orientation). By using this or a similar frame of reference, the groupworker will be able to form a useful description of at least some aspects of the life of the group.

The second requirement – some kind of explanatory theory of group processes – is much less easy to meet, but at least we can go some way in specifying the criteria that should be satisfied.

The practice of group therapy appears to provide at least

one answer. Whitaker and Lieberman[23] have discussed this issue for group therapy and it seems that much of their argument is applicable to social groupwork. This can be seen if in the following account of their discussion, groupwork is substituted for group therapy, and groupworker for group therapist. 'What is required is a theory of group processes relevant to the tasks and goals of psychotherapy. To be useful to the group therapist, a theory of group functioning must focus on factors which bear on the therapeutic process and which are subject to the influence of the practising therapist.' They suggest that the list of variables that the practitioner can influence is quite short – the size and composition of the group, its physical setting, the frequency of meeting, the provision of additional one-to-one relationships outside group meetings, and the practitioner's own participation in the group. His participation must be seen against a group situation that is in constant change, and a group theory must help the practitioner to conceptualize such changes. Whitaker and Lieberman suggests that a theory should, in particular, help the practitioner to answer the following questions:

1   What kinds of emotional issues emerge in therapy groups; how are these expressed and handled?
2   How can one conceptualize the diverse and shifting events of a single therapy session?
3   What are the long-term developmental characteristics of a therapy group?
4   In what ways does the past history of a therapy group affect its current operation?
5   What are the relationships among personality, individual behaviour and the character of the group?
6   What is the impact of the group on the patient's experience: which group conditions contribute to personal growth and which interfere?
7   How does the group therapist contribute to the patient's therapeutic experience?

This is obviously a demanding list of requirements, but despite the fact that it is difficult to find a theory that is satisfactory on all these counts, it is still important to set out the requirements as clearly as possible.

COMMUNITY WORK

This subject, like social groupwork, is receiving emphasis at the present time, though the current literature is more exhortatory than descriptive of actual achievement. Part of the emphasis seems to be at the expense of social case-work. Just as in the recent past, some sociologists have sought to achieve academic respectability by criticizing the academic credentials of social work, so some social workers now seek to establish the viability of community work by attempting to undermine the real and supposed claims of social casework. This is an unnecessary procedure, since the methods of social work are not in essential competition with each other. The main purpose of this section will be to examine what community work is.

The term 'community work' is comparatively new, succeeding and incorporating two earlier terms, community development and community organization. Community development constituted an attempt at helping people in underdeveloped countries to participate in efforts to raise standards of living and to improve the quality of social life. Community organization has been developed mainly in America, where it seems to be the name for a variety of activities. It can most helpfully be seen in terms of the more effective co-ordination of different agencies within a particular area and with co-operative planning of social policy within the area. Community work, on the other hand, combines elements of community development and community organization. Partly because of this attempted integration and partly because the term 'community' itself is such a loose and value-laden concept, we should not expect too much precision in the use of 'community work'. It has, however, now come to stand for a perspective and an approach to problems different from those adopted by social caseworkers and, to a lesser extent, social group-workers.

Two ways can be followed in the attempt to discern more clearly the nature of contemporary community work. On the one hand, we could try to see the various roles played by community workers. Alternatively, we could try to construct an idea of the problem-solving process as applied to community problems. The first approach can be illustrated from a recent account of work with community groups where the author isolates a number of roles played by the workers. The social worker in these projects participated in what are seen as group and community processes in various ways:

> As an objective observer. The role of the community development worker is that of an objective observer of the community process. Objective observation is not meant to imply any 'scientific' way of making infallible judgments about what is happening, but simply implies that his role includes attempting to 'see both sides of the story' and to help the groups to do the same.[24]

The community worker also adopts the roles of controlled participant, agent of social change and resource person. It is worth remarking that in this useful account of what community workers actually do, there does seem to be some discrepancy (noticeable in other work also) between the fairly elaborate theoretical background possessed by the workers and the kind of reasonable, sensible things the workers do. The quotation also shows some of the difficulty inherent in the attempt to demonstrate what community work (or any other method of social work) is, by suggesting what it is not. Objective observation is not clarified by the contrast drawn with a scientific way of making infallible judgments; the latter is simply not a recognizable process.

The second way of clarifying community work is to attempt to discern something in the nature of a community problem-solving process. Thus, a recent study[25] saw the community worker contributing to the following five essential phases: exploration and study, creating a structure and supports, formulating policy, implementing plans and evaluation. At each stage two connected processes are involved, those of analysis and action. For example, in the third phase, that of policy formulation, analysis consists of 'Postulating alternative goals, strategies and resources. Selecting from among alternatives for recommendation to decision-makers in the light of resistance and opportunities.' Action at this stage includes, 'Promoting expression and exchange of preferences. Testing out the feasibility of various alternatives with relevant persons. Assisting decision-makers to weigh alternatives, to choose, and to overcome resistance.'

There are obvious parallels between the processes described and those that obtain in casework, and it is tempting to suggest that as the caseworker treats the individual or family unit, so the community worker treats his community. Ross, for example, defines community organizations as,

> . . . a process by which a community identifies its needs or objectives, orders (ranks) these needs or objectives, develops the confidence and will to work at these needs or objectives, finds the resources (internal and/or external) to deal with these needs or objectives, takes action in respect of these, and in so doing extends and develops co-operative and collaborative attitudes and practices in the community.[26]

If the words 'family' or 'individual' were substituted for 'community', we would have a reasonable statement about social casework. In fact it seems that community organization or community work may take a number of different forms, some of which entail different attitudes to the helping process. As Marris and Rein indicate: [27]

> Community organization could, then, be interpreted with a very different emphasis, according to the standpoint of the organizer. It could be used to encourage the residents of a neighbourhood to come to terms with the demands of a wider society, and conversely, to force the institutions of that society to adapt more sympathetically to the special needs of a neighbourhood. Or it could be seen rather as a form of therapy, to treat apathy and social disintegra-

tion. As it might take an individual bias – promoting the social mobility of potential leaders, championing cases of personal injustices – or a communal bias more concerned with the neighbourhood as a mutually supportive community.[28]

They go on to argue later in the book that the therapeutic analogy breaks down: 'A community cannot, like an individual patient, ask for treatment and describe its symptoms. Hence it cannot initiate and ultimately control the relationship with its helper. Social therapy, therefore, tends towards a paternalism which undermines the very qualities it is seeking to promote: self-confidence and self-respect.'

This quotation suggests something of a conflict between the different technical assumptions that could be made within community work. We have seen in both social casework and social groupwork, that workers employ a range of techniques, but the kind of difference correctly identified in the case of community work cannot so easily be accommodated. It is perhaps the most important contribution of community work at the present time that it emphasizes the crucial place of conflict in understanding incompatibilities between ways of working and differences between groups and institutions in a society. Many of our social problems, argue the community workers, are the result of structural social inequalities and of conflict between social groups. They can most effectively be approached, if not solved, through major policy change, and influencing general social policy in particular directions should become part of the technical expertise of the social worker. It is, however, still an open question (though one of considerable interest for the future of social work) whether participation in policy formation can be *taught* at a technical level, and what precisely would characterize a specifically social work participation.

Some common aspects

As we have reviewed some of the important questions that

arise in a consideration of the main methods of social work, certain common features will have become apparent. First, the social worker is trying to understand the situation facing his client, whether the client is a particular family or individual, a group, or a number of groups in a community. Thus, a report on community work suggests that analyses of the activities of those using this method of social work 'do not always recognize the double task, i.e. definition of the problem by the worker and how he uses this to help the community to find its solution for itself. The analysis of the problem by the worker and by the community itself may well be different. . . .'[29] Statements about the social worker trying to understand situations may appear vacuous or coy, but they have substantive implications. In the first place, the process whereby the social worker attempts to understand the situation seems often to constitute a major element in the client's experience of being helped. As Coleridge noted, 'The unspeakable Comfort to a good man's mind – may, even to the criminal to be *understood* – to have someone that understands one – and who does not feel, that on earth, no one does.'[30] Again, social workers already claim to understand certain situations, and their clients also claim that they have been understood. We could gain considerable insight into social work if we could investigate the grounds on which such claims are made. Social workers are at present perhaps unduly influenced by the expectation that any explanation, any claim to have successfully understood something must meet 'scientific criteria'. It is important to recognize the range of explanations available (and to begin to study at which points in the range social work understanding begins to operate). Some idea of the range of explanation available can be found in the attempt by Hospers to discover an answer to the simple question: why did the water pipes break?[31] 'They always do when the temperature falls to below 32 degrees. Question two: Why do they break when the temperature falls to below 32 degrees? Explanation: Because water expands when it freezes. Question three: Why does water expand when it freezes? The answer to this question can be given in terms of the structure of the water molecule.' Hospers points out that the different explanations are all 'genuine' and that the first two explanations do not depend upon having an answer for the third question.

Second, all the methods of social work attempt to achieve their objectives through the active involvement of those being helped. Thus, for the method of social casework Mary Richmond stated:

> Human beings are not dependent and domestic animals. This fact of man's difference from other animals establishes the need of his participation in making and carrying out plans for his welfare. Individuals have wills and purposes of their own and are not fitted to play a passive part in the world; they deteriorate when they do.[32]

The function of the community worker has been described in the following terms, which underline the importance of community involvement:

> . . . to clarify priorities of social need by fact finding and by encouraging members of the community to consider their own problems and attempt to relate these to other available services. He offers to groups in the community information which will educate, inform and enable them to perceive more accurately the nature of their own problems. . . . It is clear that in encouraging members of the community to discuss their problems, in educating them as to the nature of these and in helping them to take action on their own behalf, the community worker may become engaged in political activity.[33]

Third, this involvement entails that the social worker should be constantly attending to the impact that his service is having upon the client and the client's problem. In community work evaluation of the intended and unintended consequences of the social work intervention is an essential part of the method, and if social casework is defined as a problem-solving process, it is important to recall that the final stage of such a process is usually taken to be some check that the problem has in fact been solved. This attention to the impact of social work help raises two serious problems, one psychological and the other methodological. Social workers, especially perhaps social work students, sometimes seem to act on the assumption that they should be attending to their interaction with clients in the greatest detail so that they can avoid 'the fatal' mistake, or make the decisive intervention. An annual report of the Charity Organization Society (1933/4) described and supported this assumption when it stressed the way in which practising social workers as opposed to theorists arrived at a correct method of working: 'A word or an intonation in the wrong place, or an emphasis in the right place, brought at once a flag of distress, anger, warning, or gratitude into the answering eyes.' Social work is a more robust kind of intervention than this.

The other difficulty, the methodological, concerns the difficulties raised for the appraisal of social work intervention by the ways in which social workers consistently define both the problems and the reactions of their clients. We have seen in the discussion of social groupwork, for example, that a social worker may well understand an incident in the life of a group without necessarily sharing her perception with the group. Similarly, the 'diagnosis' of the problem facing a group in the community may not coincide with that made by the community worker. It is within this context that critics of social work ask, 'Do we know with any certainty what the client thinks he is doing in the interview? Is this not frankly a form of quasi-captive psychotherapy done in the name of advancing the professionalization of social work, but largely in ignorance of the attitudes and definitions of one of the two participants? . . .'[34] This criticism is directed largely at one of the methods we have discussed, social casework, but social workers generally should take seriously the idea that they form one of the types of persons who in the words of Wright Mills, are trained 'to think in terms of "situations". Their activities and mental outlook are set within the existent norms of society; in their professional work they tend to have an occupationally trained incapacity to rise above series of

THE METHODS OF SOCIAL WORK

"cases".'[35] And, the argument could be continued, rising above such series is a necessary condition for understanding some or all of a social agency's clients.

As the methods can be said to share the possibility of a common criticism, so – and this is the fourth common element – they share a difficulty in establishing a firm identity. Thus, it might be argued groupwork could be absorbed without noticeable remainder into education and group psychotherapy; casework could be absorbed into individual psychotherapy and social service administration, which with the help of political action might also take over community work. Yet this 'tidy' solution to the problem of identity (abolish the source of the problem) would, if the argument of this book is valid, destroy the possibility of future exploration and therapeutic endeavour (in the widest sense), which is valuable precisely because it is on so many important boundaries.

NOTES

[1] From an unsigned article entitled 'God's Puppets', *Charity Organisation Quarterly*, April 1924.
[2] Webb, B., *My Apprenticeship*, London: Longmans, 1926, p. 206.
[3] ibid., p. 206 *n.1*.
[4] ibid, p. 197.
[5] ibid., p. 205.
[6] Bosanquet, B., *Rich and Poor*, London: Macmillan, 1896, p. 6.
[7] ibid., p. 210.
[8] Definition quoted in *Report* of the (Younghusband) Working Party on Social Workers in The Local Authority Health and Welfare Services S. 638, 1959.
[9] Perlman, H., 'Casework Is Dead?', *Social Casework*, January 1967.
[10] Source untraceable.
[11] Miss Lyons, 'The Art of Helping', *Charity Organisation Society Occasional Papers*, 4th Series, No. 17, 1908.
[12] Charity Organization Review, Jan. 1902.
[13] *Annual Report* of the C.O.S. 1933/4.
[14] Bosanquet, B., 'The Meaning of Social Work', *International Journal of Ethics*, April 1901.
[15] Parsloe, P., 'Some Thoughts on Social Group Work', *British Journal of Psychiatric Social Work*, Spring 1969.

114

[16] Hollis, F., *Social Casework: A Psycho-Social Therapy*, New York: Random House, 1964.

[17] Shalinsky, W., 'Group Composition as an Element of Social Group Work Practice', *Social Service Review*, March 1969.

[18] McWhinnie, A., 'Group Counselling with Adoptive Families', *Case Conference*, March 1968.

[19] Homans, G., *The Human Group*, London: Routledge & Kegan Paul, 1957.

[20] Bion, W., *Experiences in Groups*, London: Tavistock, 1961.

[21] Sherwood, M., 'Bion's Experiences in Groups: a Critical Evaluation', *Human Relations*, XVII, no. 2., 1964.

[22] Benne, K., and Sheats, P., 'Functional Roles of Group Members', *Journal of Social Issues*, IV, Spring 1948.

[23] Whitaker, S., and Lieberman, M., *Psychotherapy through the Group Process*, New York: Atherton Press, 1964, pp. 7-8.

[24] Goetschius, G., *Working with Community Groups*, London: Routledge & Kegan Paul, 1969, p. 174.

[25] *Community Work and Social Change*, London: Longmans, 1968, pp. 68-9.

[26] Ross, M. G., *Community Organisation – Theory and Principles*, New York: Harper, 1955, p. 92.

[27] Marris, P., and Rein, M., *Dilemmas of Social Reform*, London: Routledge & Kegan Paul, 1967, p. 169.

[28] ibid., p. 189.

[29] *Community Work and Social Change*, op. cit., p. 67.

[30] Coleridge, S. T., *Notebooks*, I, 1082. 6., London: Routledge & Kegan Paul, 1962.

[31] Hospers, J., 'Explanations', in *Essays in Conceptual Analysis*, ed. A. Flew, London: Macmillan, 1930.

[32] Richmond, M., *What is Social Casework?*, New York: Russell Sage Foundation, 1922, p. 258.

[33] *Community Work and Social Change*, op. cit., p. 70.

[34] Kuhn, M., 'The Interview and The Professional Relationship', in *Human Behaviour and Social Processes*, ed. A. Rose, London: Routledge & Kegan Paul, 1962.

[35] Wright Mills, C., 'The Professional Ideology of Social Pathologists', *American Journal of Sociology*, September 1943.

5

Social Work Values

VALUES ALWAYS RECEIVE a somewhat reverential treatment in social work literature, probably too much so. It is difficult to find a social work text that does not devote considerable space to the principles of social work. Thus, *Introduction to a Social Worker* states: 'The ethical values which underlie casework are: to respect the client, to accept him for himself, not to condemn him, to uphold the right to self-determination, and to respect his confidence.'[1] To take another example from community work, Murray Ross has stated:

> The value orientation of community organization (and, indeed, of all social work) derives from acceptance of certain concepts and facts as a foundation for work with people. Among these articles of faith are: the essential dignity and ethical worth of the individual, the possession by each individual of potentialities and resources for managing his own life, the importance of freedom to express one's individuality, the great capacity for growth within all social beings, the right of the individual to those basic physical necessities (food, shelter, and clothing) without which fulfilment of life is often blocked, the need for the individual to struggle and strive to improve his own life and environment, the right of the individual to help in time of need and crisis, the importance of a social organization for which the individual feels responsible and which is responsive to individual feeling, the need of a social climate which encourages individual growth and development, the right and responsibility of the individual to participate in the affairs of his community, the practicability of discussion, conference, and consulta-

tion as methods for the solution of individual and social problems, 'self-help' as the essential basis of any programme of aid etc.

These and other similar orientations constitute the 'bias' of social work, condition its goals, and preclude certain types of action felt to be more useful by its critics.[2]

These two quotations clearly illustrate the list-making approach common in the treatment of the values of social work. Such an approach painstakingly decreases the likelihood of argument, and argument is required rather than the existing almost catechetical method. What kinds of argument should be developed? This question is obviously far-reaching and complex and in this introductory work it will not be possible to treat the issue systematically. What is possible is the discussion of illustrative questions. Consequently, we shall review some of the research conducted into the values social workers hold, and examine some of the many complex problem situations which they have to face and within whose context they often have to act. The problem of the consistency of social work values will be approached through the examination of one particular concept on which social workers seem to lay great stress, namely self-determination. Finally, the issue of implicit values will be illustrated by considering the value of professionalism, which often seems to represent an objective for social workers, even though the values inherent in professionalism are often left implicit.

THE VALUES OF SOCIAL WORKERS

A number of assumptions are often made in discussion of the values upheld (or realized by) social workers. For example, it is assumed that the values in question are those to be found listed in the different texts or that social workers in fact share the same values. Both these assumptions are questioned in a recent study by McLeod and Meyer[3] which seeks to discover whether or not social workers differ amongst themselves in regard to values, and whether they uphold values that are in some ways different from those held by other professions. First, however, they attempted to ask the question: how can we describe the values that social workers hold? Instead of relying on one or more of the available lists they abstracted from social work literature ten value dimensions as follows: individual work v. system goals ('within our society there are those who tend to favour the individual and those who tend to favour the group in situations where conflict of interests occurs'); personal liberty v. society control; group responsibility v. individual responsibility; security satisfaction v. struggle, suffering and denial; relativism, pragmatism v. absolution, sacredness; innovation, change v. traditionalism; diversity v. homogeneity; cultural determinism v. inherent human nature; interdependence v. individual autonomy; individualization v. stereotyping. The authors argue that social workers tend to take up a position along each of these dimensions, but before discussing the results of applying their Social Values Test, we should note the importance of clarity and accuracy of the description of value positions. Thus, in the descriptions used values are once again built in. For example, innovation/change seems opposed to traditionalism, but one must reflect that a man may be traditionalist in his acknowledgement of a response to change rather than in his 'blind' resistance to it. Moreover, a man may be a traditionalist in some things and a radical in many others. Hobbes, Coleridge, Hume, and Newman are good examples in the fields of philosophy and theology. So, whilst we welcome the attempt to arrive at a statement of the values of social work by examining what social workers write as distinct from what others suggest on their behalf, it is true that the area of social work values, like so many aspects of social work, requires not only rigorous empirical enquiry but also hard conceptual exploration.

When the Social Values Test was applied to the responses of the social workers it was found that 7 out of the 10 items were significantly related to the level of professional training in the expected direction (i.e., towards the first dimension named in each pair). In order of decreasing relationship these items were: security-satisfaction v. struggle, suffering and denial; group responsibility v. individual responsibility; interdependence v. individual autonomy; cultural determinism v. inherent human nature; individual worth v. systems goals; diversity v. homogeneity. There were only small differences between the trained social workers and the students in training, but social workers with a religious faith scored highly on all the value dimensions regardless of their training status. This last observation indicates one of the difficulties of study in this area, namely the extent to which 'social work' values overlap with, or even express, those deriving from a range of other sources. It is also worth noting that these value dimensions are expressed in a very abstract manner, and it might well be the case that many other groups besides social workers would espouse the particular emphasis we have been discussing. To some extent this has been shown by further research by Meyer, Litwak and Warren[4] who compared the values of social workers with those of teachers. They started from the assumption that social workers and teachers occupied the same rank in the social class hierarchy though their work situation and objectives were quite distinct. Did this difference create a different set of values for each profession? They took five of the dimensions already used and found that on all five values social workers preferred the first named value position whilst the teachers chose the second. However, when the group of over 700 teachers was analysed in terms of a distinction between primary and secondary school teachers, it was found that the values of the primary school teachers closely resembled those of the social workers.

Another attempt to examine the problem empirically was made by Pumphrey, who collected and analysed 'words used in social work technical treatises offered as assignments, words used by teachers and students in classes audited, and words in project questionnaires and correspondence which seemed to express value or ethical prescriptions. . . .'[5] She noted the values most frequently mentioned. As a result she was able to draw up a list of values divided in terms of three different levels, highly abstract, middle-range and instrumental. The first category included the following: each human being should be regarded by all others as an object of infinite worth; he should be preserved in a state commensurate with his innate dignity and protected from suffering; human betterment is possible, the most effective changes cannot be imposed; much concerning man is knowable. In the middle range of values Pumphrey mentions intermediate goals for the social worker revolving around concepts of the well-functioning person, the 'good' family, and the 'growth-enhancing' group. Instrumental values are concerned with the idea of the 'good' professional, who is under an obligation always to seek a whole view of man, who should be a warm, non-blaming person, who perceives himself as someone who communicates, preserves and changes norms.

The kind of distinction that Pumphrey uses is one that social workers may well find useful in their discussion and analysis of values, but the content of some of her examples requires further analysis. For instance, it is somewhat puzzling to be told that 'each human being should be regarded by all others as an object of infinite worth', because it is difficult to be sure what counts as 'regarding someone' in this way. Presumably some lines of conduct are ruled out if we subscribe to this value (e.g., don't kick a man when he's down, or, come to that, up) but this kind of behaviour could be ruled out by much less abstract propositions. Similarly, are social workers sure that they should *protect* people from suffering, when their activities suggest other values that might well conflict with this? *Protective* activity might sometimes clash with the client's right of self-determination, whilst suffering could be said to be part of 'the reality' which social workers quite often believe they should assist their clients to face.

It seems in fact much more profitable to conduct the study of social work values not so much on the basis of the values social workers mention, but on what they actually do when faced with a choice between valued courses of action. The question to ask is not so much what things, concepts, states of affairs, do social workers value, but how much do they value them. And this can only be discovered when social workers have to put their values in some order of priority. As Taylor has remarked in connection with the values of those teaching in teacher-training colleges:

> Short of systematic enquiry in depth among large numbers of college teachers it is very difficult to establish what are the dominant values; without careful institutional studies it is impossible to state how these values are represented in action; and without much more thorough-going and sophisticated follow-up studies than have been undertaken to date, it is difficult to say what effects the value systems of the colleges have upon the development of students and the manner in which they work in the school.[6]

Some problem situations

In the following set of examples taken mainly from the records of social workers a number of problem situations have been selected, some apparently very simple, others more complex. They have been chosen to illustrate both the problems social workers face as part of their job and also as situations in which the social workers feel, whether correctly or not, that they are in conflict about what they should do. They are offered as possible bases for discussion, and not as illustrations of the most urgent problems in values or as pegs on which firm general conclusions can be hung:

1. A severely subnormal man, *John X* (35), doubly incontinent, lived with his aged parents (m.65 and f.70) in a deserted country cottage with no running water. His parents have never had a holiday. They refuse to apply for a vacancy in a hostel and insist on caring for their son, though this is undermining their physical and mental health and they are tending to 'neglect' the mother's sister (60) who is also living with them.

Should the social worker try to persuade the parents to apply for a vacancy and if so, with what justification?

2. *Edgar B.* (18) was reared in very unhappy home circumstances with parents constantly quarrelling. He reacted with violent outbursts of temper and was taken to a child guidance clinic at the age of fourteen. A psychologist stated his I.Q. was 89. On leaving school he had a variety of jobs and it was found that when unemployed police and social workers were constantly called into the home because of Edgar's violent tempers which included smashing up the home and beating his mother. He was admitted to the local mental hospital for two short periods as an informal patient and also joined a travelling circus for a month but the basic problem still remained. He joined the army but was discharged after eight weeks. On returning home he was unemployed for three weeks and his tempers once again became uncontrollable and among other things he smashed a window at his home. Suitable employment could not be obtained but eventually he found a job with an army depot packing army equipment. On the very first day he brought home two bayonets and when playing with a thirteen-year-old girl that evening, slightly cut two fingers of her hand. He apparently took the bayonets back two days later.

The social worker saw the problem as follows:
(1) If the police and army were informed, Edgar would certainly be sacked and the violent behaviour at home would continue perhaps indefinitely;
(2) Would a severe warning with the hope that there would be no repetition be the better course in view of all the circumstances?

Has the social worker correctly described the problem and what are the circumstances he should consider before deciding on the better course?

3. *Mr B.* (25) and *Mrs B.* (22) were first known to the children's department when they applied to a local moral welfare worker to act as foster parents to illegitimate babies prior to their placement for adoption. The child care officer visited and on the first occasion met only Mrs B. who told her that they were hoping to apply to an adoption society themselves but at the moment were awaiting medical certi-

ficates from their doctor who was having to obtain past medical history as they had only recently moved to the area. Mrs B. also mentioned that they had known for two years that Mr B. was infertile, but she said that she felt sure that he was worried about talking about this, particularly when it came to the point of their applications to an adoption society. A few weeks later the C.C.O. visited again and met Mr B. as well on this occasion. Mrs B. told the C.C.O. that plans were afoot for her to attend a gynaecologist with a view to undergoing A.I.D. (artificial insemination by donor). They were not sure whether they would, in fact, do this and they were anxious to learn as much as possible about it from the C.C.O. A few weeks later a baby was placed with Mr and Mrs B. by the moral welfare worker as a temporary arrangement before being placed in an adoptive home. They were visited within ten days of placement of the baby and Mrs B. appeared to be very attached to him and said that it would break her husband's heart when the baby went. Within another four weeks Mr B. came into the office to say that he and his wife had decided to adopt this baby who had been placed with them under a private arrangement with his mother, who had given verbal agreement. He said that his wife was seeing the gynaecologist and would continue to do so. The Bs. then gave official notification of their intention to adopt the baby and welfare supervision visits started. About three months later the moral welfare worker mentioned to the C.C.O. that she thought Mrs B. was pregnant. The C.C.O. visited and almost immediately upon her arrival Mrs B. told her that she was pregnant and discussed some of her feelings and those of her husband about this. She obviously had very mixed feelings about this coming baby. She mentioned that only one relative knew that she had been undergoing A.I.D. and that the rest of the family would not know of this. The visit was in fact towards the end of the welfare supervision period.

In the area in which the family live the probation officer is normally appointed as Guardian ad Litem and it was here that considerable difficulties arose with regard to *professional conduct*. It was eventually decided that the G.A.L.

should not be told by the C.C.O. that Mrs B. was pregnant by A.I.D. and the family knew that this would be a matter for them to mention or not, as they saw fit. In fact they did tell the G.A.L. of this. The C.C.O. suggested that she would have been in a considerable quandary had she been appointed as G.A.L. and thought it likely that she would not have mentioned it, on the basis that while absolute secrecy about such matters is by no means a good thing; nevertheless it seemed that the state of public opinion being what it was, it was important that the child should not know of its method of conception and therefore the officer would have to play her part in hiding the fact too.

4. The psychiatric social worker received a letter from a client she was seeing as an out-patient of the mental hospital. The letter expressed the client's worries about God's will: 'God has become someone terrible who must be answered. And I've got no answer, only failure.' The P.S.W. replied that she knew how hard the client had been trying and that she was quite sure that in the long run this would not be in vain: 'We all have times when we hate people, but this does not mean that we are bad or failures, and surely God knows about this and understands. Sometimes it does look as if He asks the impossible of us, but perhaps it is because we are often more severe on ourselves than He is – and that we underrate His capacity for love and forgiveness.' In the interview following this exchange of letters the P.S.W. referred to Christ's Agony in the Garden.

In this extract the conflict would be between those social workers who believe they should try to use the client's own value system and those who would avoid this on principle.

5. *Mr and Mrs A.* had two children *Jane (4½) and Mary (1)*. Jane presented worrying behaviour – no speech, unsteady gait, clinging and almost continually crying. A good deal of consultation went on between the family doctor, the head-mistress of the nursery school, the speech therapist who had seen Jane but had not been able to work with her as yet, the assistant medical officer of health, who had tried to

assess her intelligence, and the health visitor! It was generally agreed that, although it was quite possible that Jane
might be mentally sub-normal, this was most probably, or
equally as likely, to be an emotional disorder, and it was
felt that no definite diagnosis should be made for some
time. This was explained to Mrs A., who accepted a 'wait
and see' policy quite well. After Jane had been about a
year at the nursery school, there was little progress with
speech, although she appeared to be more secure and did
not cry so much. Because it was felt there was much
emotional disturbance in both parents and child, the
case was referred to the child guidance clinic. The health
visitor first discussed the case with the P.S.W. at the
clinic.

The child was seen once at the clinic, she was very upset
and cried and clung to her mother. The psychiatrist thought
that Jane was definitely mentally sub-normal, and told Mrs
A. that she should accept this, explaining that it was in no
way her fault. Mrs A. says that she came home in a very
distressed state. She told the nursery school headmistress
about the interview, saying what a shock it was, she would
never go back to the child guidance centre, but who was
she to believe, etc., etc. The headmistress reported to the
health visitor, who contacted the family doctor, so that they
could both take the same line and avoid being placed in a
position of criticism towards their colleagues.

There was a considerable problem of loyalty to the child
guidance team whilst trying to keep Mrs A. from losing faith
again in her advisers and slipping into despair and hopeless-
ness. The child guidance team explained to the health
visitor that they felt it was better for Mrs A. to realize and
accept Jane's limitations and stop feeling guilty about having been the possible cause of an emotional disorder, rather
than to expect too much and be disappointed later. They
suggested seeing the child again in a year.

6. A case which was recently reported in the press illustrates
in dramatic form the complex value difficulties which often
face social workers in any field of work:

The parents of a girl, aged 12, who was stated to have taken part in nude witchcraft ceremonies, were bound over in a recognizance of £100 each to exercise proper care and guardianship over her. An education official brought the case because it was felt that the girl was exposed to moral danger. A detective sergeant said he interviewed people who had taken part in witchcraft ceremonies at the parents' home. He also interviewed the parents, who regarded the ceremonies as part of a religion known as the Wicca. He found that the child had been in the nude and present at some of the ceremonies. From his inquiries he had no doubt that excessive drinking of alcoholic liquor had been a recognized feature of the ceremonies, but as far as the child was concerned the parents alleged, she would only have a drink of Baby Moussec. He said that the girl was well cared and well provided for in the material sense. The court ordered that the girl should be placed under the supervision of a probation officer for three years.

7. Increasing uneasiness is experienced by some social workers at the power of organizations in defining what constitutes a social problem and the apparently appropriate ways of dealing with it. Such power creates or demonstrates complex problems of value. Some of these are illustrated in the following quotation from a recent report on community work:

Organizations with broad purposes select from time to time specific social problems on which to work. The character of these also shapes a community worker's activities. The very way in which an organization defines a problem situation suggests certain kinds of activities and excludes others. One would not expect a child care officer who is promoting a family advice centre to mobilize a public protest against council members opposed to the idea.[7]

The expectation seems based on a good estimate of likely behaviour, but is such behaviour on the part of the child care officer justified, and if it is, on what grounds?

Similar difficulties can be discerned in a quotation from a book describing actual projects undertaken with community groups:

> The values and standards of the agency and its workers may also conflict with those of the group. For example, a group may decide to raise money by a method of gambling which is only just on the right side of the law; or it may decide to spend money lavishly on something which professional workers may think unnecessary. A more complex situation arises when the field worker supports a group in a course of action from which his agency must dissociate itself.[8]

An example of such action could be a decision by a local group to occupy as squatters empty houses and make them over for the use of homeless families.

Self-determination

This principle is almost universally asserted in social work texts, but, because social work writers so often concentrate myopically upon social work itself, ignoring the fact that terms in social work often have a reference much wider than social work, we have only recently come to see some of its complexity. If we reflect upon the term we easily discover that it also has a use in political thought, that reference to 'self-determination' of peoples is probably as frequent as that to the self-determination of clients. The fact that a commentator in political theory has referred to this as 'the most delusive and dangerous of catchwords',[9] might have alerted us more generally to the fact that the usage of the same term in social work might not be without its difficulties, especially when the term has become something of a catchword.

Biestek in a much used text describes self-determination in social casework as follows:

The principle of client self-determination is the practical recognition of the right and need of clients to freedom in making their own choices and decisions in the casework process. Caseworkers have a corresponding duty to respect that right, recognize that need, stimulate and help to activate that potential for self-direction by helping the client to see and use the available and appropriate resources of the community and its own personality. The client's right to self determination, however, is limited by the client's capacity for positive and constructive decision making, by the framework of civil and moral law, and by the function of the agency.[10]

This is a statement of the position with which many social workers would probably agree, but there are others who see the principle somewhat differently. Some, for instance, would take a much less individualistic focus. Thus, Bernstein argues that the social worker 'ought to be a kind of social conscience which helps the client to relate his self-determination to all those with whom he has relationships. To do anything else would contribute to social degeneration'.[11] Others would argue that the kind of formulation given to the principle by Biestek qualifies the principle so much that it perhaps ceases to be a principle at all. One of the writers most vigorously arguing this position is Keith-Lucas[12] who has discerned two elements in the so-called principle of client self-determination: client participation in the operation of social treatment and non-interference on the part of the worker except in the case of essentials. Thus, instead of saying that some kinds of social work (e.g., work with neglectful parents) requires a 'realistic re-definition of the right of self-determination', it is simpler to argue that in such cases social work intervention is required at a much earlier stage than is necessary in working with other kinds of client.

This may seem like a simple matter of dispute about the way in which statements are made, but it is more significant.

Discussion of the different ways social work writers define the principle suggests that whilst they might all agree to abide by the principle it would in fact entail different kinds of behaviour on the part of the social worker. The basic difference perhaps is between those who accept social work as a means of social control, and who allow the social worker to judge under what circumstances rights may be upheld or suspended, and those who see the process of self-determination as 'often intolerably painful to the individual and to society' and not 'within our power to concede or refuse as a social benefit'.[13] These two different views are to be found throughout social work theorizing in one form or another. That they can be held by people using what seem to be the same terms, indicates the ambiguous nature of much social work theorizing: it can be interpreted in a conservative or in a more radical sense.

SOCIAL WORK AS A PROFESSION

One important aspect of social work activity that sometimes escapes critical discussion is the claim to professional status. The claim itself is often assumed: social work *is* a profession and therefore it has certain (valuable) characteristics. The claim is not often discussed within the context of values, though it is often paraded. Most social workers want professional status and the valued position in society that this constitutes and the claim is a claim to have already achieved certain values. What are these values?

This is to ask for a definition of a profession, for the essential criteria that distinguish a professional occupation from other forms of work. Several attempts have been made to describe the criteria with particular reference to social work. The first and the best-known is the early attempt by Flexner (1915).[14]

Flexner began his consideration of the question 'Is Social Work a Profession?' by admitting a genuine doubt concerning his competence to discuss the subject and a disposition not to press his conclusions too far. Yet his treatment of the question was for long considered decisive, and his discussion has been the starting point, the yardstick and the mainstay of discussions of the subject since. A professional, argued Flexner, was the opposite of the amateur, someone who spends his entire time on an activity. The term can be strictly applied only when a number of criteria are met, but there is always the danger that in stipulating these criteria we shall be arbitrary, simply choosing our own favoured characteristics, or unhistorical, relying on those features that are common to the contemporary profession. In spite of these difficulties Flexner identified six criteria, all of which had to be met, if an occupation was, in his view, to be given professional status. First, the activities involved must be essentially intellectual. Tools or manual work were not excluded but any 'instrument is an incident or an accident; the real character of the activity is a thinking process. A free, resourceful, and unhampered intelligence applied to problems and seeking to understand and master them. . . .' Second, responsibility in the occupation is large and personal because the problems that the 'professional' seeks to solve are complicated. A 'professional' is not 'under orders: though he be co-operating with others, though the work be team work, rather than individual work, his responsibility is not less complete and not less personal'. Third, professionals do not rely on knowledge or experience that is generally available. They need in Flexner's view, to resort to the laboratory or to the seminar for a constantly fresh supply of facts. Fourth, professional activities are definitely practical activities. The ends of professional work are not, of course necessarily tangible or physical, but 'the professional man must have an absolutely definite and practical object'. Fifth, a profession is a brotherhood. Lastly, professionals possess an intellectually communicable skill.

Using these criteria against a number of occupations Flexner is able to conclude that they do at least partly distinguish some occupations from others. Thus, the nursing 'profession' possesses a number of the criteria, but the nurse's function appears to be instrumental: '. . . when all is said and done it is the physician who observes, reflects and decides'. Social workers again possess some of the criteria: the activities are not mechanical or routine, but '. . . the very variety of the situations he encounters compels him to be not a professional agent so much as the mediator invoking this or that professional activity'. Social work, moreover, has no definite or specific ends: 'It appears not so much a definite field as an aspect of work in many fields.' If, for example, medicine was fully socialized, medical men and medical institutions might well look after certain interests that the medical social worker has to care for at present, simply because of the short fall of medical practice. Finally, Flexner found it difficult to envisage an educational preparation for social work that would be worthy of a profession: '. . . the occupations of social workers are so numerous and diverse that no compact, purposeful, organized educational discipline is feasible. Well-informed, well-balanced, tactful, judicious, sympathetic, resourceful people are needed, rather than any definite kind or kinds of technical skill.' It is not surprising that Flexner concluded that the reward of social status connected with a professional identity was not to be conferred on the social work: '. . . the rewards of the social worker are in his conscience and in heaven.'

A number of comments can be made. First, Flexner's description of a profession is, like so many descriptions since, an implicit hymn of praise to 'the professional', and it is difficult to disentangle commendation from description. In other words a profession is a good thing, and for a number of good reasons, each one of which constitutes a criterion for being professional.

Second, whilst his argument would need revision in a number of respects it is still powerful. It gently chides the social worker, and this can be taken as a reminder that when the question is raised 'Is social work a profession?' it is important to see this as a question connected with the movement of a considerable number of occupations to achieve professional status and an identity. A discussion of the professional nature of social work must be conducted within a wider framework. Flexner's questioning of what would now be described as the knowledge base of social work is still important. Thus, a more recent discussion[15] suggests that occupational groups in the process of professionalization must be able to avoid a situation in which their knowledge is either too broad or too vague. The author suggests that this constitutes the dilemma of most human relationship professions.

Third, and this is where Flexner's discussion begins to carry less weight, we should recognize that the question to ask is not if social work is a profession – in the end such a question will be redundant since it will or will not be so recognized. Rather there are two questions: how professionalized has an occupation or parts of an occupation become; what professional model is it trying to emulate?

There are two main approaches to the first question, the analytic and the historical. The analytic approach attempts to establish the essential attributes of professional behaviour and on this basis to define a scale of professionalism. Thus, Hickson and Thomas[16] propose the following four essential attributes: generalized knowledge; primary orientation to the community interest; internalized codes of ethics, and rewards which primarily symbolize work achievement. Using these attributes social work would not, it seems, have a high place on a scale of professionalism. The other approach to the question can be illustrated from Wilensky's recent attempt to outline the natural history of professionalization.[17] He suggests that a typical process of professionalization can be identified. Men begin to do the work in question on a full-time basis and start to stake-out a jurisdiction, some boundaries of competence; the early masters of the technique or adherents of the movement become concerned about standards of training and practice and they establish a training school which within two or three decades makes academic connections with a university, if it is not already established within one; the teachers and practitioners then achieve success in promoting more effective professional organizations. Towards the end of the process legal monopoly of the skill is sought and, finally, a formal code of ethics is adopted.

At any stage in such a process the advance towards professionalization may be halted by difficulties that pose problems of value. Thus, in relation to social work it has been observed that the development of 'the profession' largely within the context of large governmental bureaucracies constitutes a threat to 'professional autonomy'. In order to understand this problem, however, in its full significance, it is once again necessary to go outside the confines of social work practice and recognize those features of the problem that reflect a more general social problem. Sometimes social workers see the problem simply in sloganistic terms as a choice between being made 'organization men', who carry out the orders and maintain the beliefs and values of 'the system', and becoming 'the clients' man'. But the problem social workers face is part of the wider social problem of the clash between authority that claims to be professional and authority resting on some other basis. King[18] has suggested three possible responses of the professional in the face of this conflict; each response has in fact been adopted by social workers at different points of time, and each has different value implications. In the first place the professional may narrow his claim to autonomy, so that he tacitly or explicitly surrenders authority to lay down the general lines on which his work should be done and rests content with a claim in respect of the detailed implementation of policy in his field. This, suggests King, is the position of the professional soldier who surrenders strategy to the layman, whilst claiming expertise in respect of tactics. Alternatively, the professional can attempt to expand effective power beyond the sphere of traditionally recognized expertise. 'As practitioners they inevitably have an influence upon the implementation of policy in their fields of practice whatever role they play in its formulation. As a result, even where they no longer participate directly in general policy-making, they continue to exercise a limited veto over proposals that can be put into effect only with their co-operation.' Thirdly, the professional instead of working towards the creation of effective power can attempt the redefinition of his expertise, so that a range of political and administrative skills are included within the confines of professional expertise. Such a redefinition, King remarks, is not easy to secure. It meets resistance both from 'purists' within the profession itself who wish to preserve its special character, and so argue that the professional and political or administrative lives and perspectives are fundamentally at variance with one another, and from outsiders whose interests lies in having professional expertise, as the phrase goes, 'on tap but not on top'.

So far we have been considering some of the implications that arise from asking one of the two questions it was earlier suggested were crucial in the discussion of social work as a profession, namely how professionalized social work has become as an occupation. The second question, that of what professional model social work is trying to copy, again involves issues in which it is difficult to disentangle factual from value considerations. As a matter of historical fact it is probably true to say, as does Wilensky,[19] that social work has vacillated between two models of a profession, the ministry (with the emphasis on social reform based on doctrine) and medicine (with the emphasis on scientifically based clinical practice). We can begin to consider which is the most appropriate model or whether different aspects of social work require different models, only when we have described in much more detail than at present the two main models and drawn out their implications. Thus, it is possible to interpret the ministry model in at least two different senses. The 'doctrine' involved could be based on a disillusionment with large-scale political solutions to social problems. This seems to be the assumption of at least one important attempt to describe the *faith* of the counselling professions.[20] Alternatively, the 'doctrine' could be of a general utopian kind seeking the realization of the 'Kingdom' in the immediate transformation of social relationships.

CONCLUSION

Sociology has had difficulty in deciding whether or not it can be 'value free'. To a lesser extent the same kind of trouble has arisen in social work. It has been assumed that the caseworker simply helps people to realize themselves, that the group worker helps the group to implement its purpose, that the community worker helps the neighbourhood come to a sense of its identity and then takes some kind of corporate action. The means – casework, groupwork, etc. – are seen as 'neutral'. But in this human activity it is difficult if not impossible to separate the ends from the means and it is rare for the ends to be achieved, whereas the means are 'always happening'. Moreover, it is now coming to be recognized that whilst the social worker is client-focused this does not always entail attending on the consensus. As Simey has recently stated in regard to social workers: 'It is by no means sufficient for them to guide their actions only by getting to know what the consensus of opinion is on one issue or another. There are occasions on which they must lead rather than follow.'[21] However, Simey shares with social work literature a silence on how we can decide when such occasions have arisen and what entitles us to judge when the leadership has been well or badly exercised.

NOTES

[1] *Introduction to a Social Worker*, Allen & Unwin, 1964.

[2] Ross, M., *Community Organisation: Theory and Principles*, Harper, 1955, p. 78.

[3] McLeod, D., and Meyer, H., 'A study of the Values of Social Workers', *Behavioural Science for Social Workers*, ed. E. J. Thomas, New York: Collier-Macmillan, 1967.

[4] Meyer, H., Litwak E., and Warren, D., 'Occupational and Class Differences in Social Values: A Comparison of Teachers and Social Workers', *Sociology of Education*, Vol. 41, no. 3, Summer 1968.

[5] Pumphrey, M., *The Teaching of Values and Ethics in Social Work Education*, Council for Social Work Education – Social work Curriculum Study No. 13, 1959, p. 25.

[6] Taylor, W., *Society and the Education of Teachers*, London: Faber, 1969, p. 271.

[7] *Community Work and Social Change*, London: Longmans, 1968, p. 65.

[8] Goetschius, G., *Working with Community Groups,* London: Routledge & Kegan Paul, 1969, p. 150.

[9] Shuri, M., *The Concept of Self-Determination in the United Nations,* Damascus Al Jadidah Press, 1965.

[10] Biestek, F., *The Casework Relationship,* London: Allen & Unwin, 1961, p. 103.

[11] Bernstein, S., 'Self-Determination: King or Citizen in the Realm of Values', *Social Work* (U.S.A.), v., no. 1, January 1960.

[12] Keith Lucas, B., 'A Critique of the Principle of Client Self-Determination', *Social Work* (U.S.A.), VIII, No. 3, July 1963.

[13] Marcus, G., 'The Status of Social Casework Today', *Readings in Social Case Work 1920-1938,* New York: Columbia University Press, 1939.

[14] Flexner, A., 'Is Social Work a Profession?', *Proceedings of the 42nd National Conference of Charities and Correction,* 1915.

[15] Wilensky, H., 'The Professionalisation of Everyone', *American Journal of Sociology,* LXX, No. 2, Sept. 1964.

[16] Hickson, D., and Thomas, M., 'Professionalisation in Britain', *Sociology,* III, No. 1, January 1969.

[17] Wilensky, H., op. cit.

[18] King, M. D., 'Science and the Professional Dilemma', *Penguin Social Sciences Survey 1968,* ed. J. Gould.

[19] Wilensky, op. cit.

[20] Halmos, P., *The Faith of the Counsellors,* London: Constable, 1965.

[21] Simey, T. S., *Social Science and Social Purpose,* London: Constable, 1968, p. 195.

6

Education for Social Work

THIS CHAPTER DEALS with the main developments in social work education and describes the present rather complex position. It then discusses some of the problems that arise within the three main roles involved in this educational process: the fieldwork teacher, the academic staff, and the student.

THE DEVELOPMENT AND PRESENT POSITION OF SOCIAL WORK EDUCATION

The social work of the nineteenth century was typically amateur. The nineteenth-century 'social worker' – the term itself does not become common until the turn of the century – was a middle-class man or woman who tried to befriend the unfortunate. 'What the poor most want', wrote S. R. Bosanquet, in the first half of the century, 'is a friend. They want more notice, and attention, and communication.'[1] His view was echoed later in Kingsley's novel *Yeast* (1851), in which agricultural workers are offered ultimate hope in a new generation of 'young gentlemen' who would become 'the guides and the guardians of the labouring men'. It was partly this same kind of hope which led to the foundation of the Settlements later in the century, when certain groups became convinced that 'To shut one's self away from that half of the race life, [which was concerned with the struggle against starvation] is to shut one's self away from the most vital part of it; it is to live out but half the humanity which we have been born heir to and to use but half our faculties'.[2]

What constitutes a common element in all these hopes and schemes is the assumption that social work required no special training, that the sharing of what the well-to-do already had – 'social tact and training . . . the tradition and custom of hospitality'[3] – would be sufficient. If the wealthy 'social worker' needed guidance on the practical detail of his philanthropy he was urged, in the manuals then current, to reflect on his own family experience or on his own dealings with his servants.

It was in the 1890s that this amateur tradition began to give way before the growing conviction that the practice of social work required some kind of systematic training and personal preparation. This belief was first expressed in the social work agency. Helen Bosanquet, for example, in 1900 stressed as her main principle in training,

> . . . that we keep the student [who came to the C.O.S.], from falling into anything like conventionality. Conventional ways of classifying cases, conventional modes of help, conventional rules for making inquiries, all are dangerous, and especially dangerous in our work. It is comparatively easy to learn the little list of categories: *Not likely to benefit, Left to Clergy, Poor Law case, Necessary information refused,* and to class our case under it; what is more important and difficult is to learn how to keep it out of these classes, and this requires an insight to which every case is unique and individual.[4]

By 1890 the Women's University Settlement in Southwark had already joined forces with Octavia Hill, who began the first training scheme for her own housing workers, and the Charity Organization Society was developing its own ideas about training. In 1902 an important conference was called to discuss the part that the universities might play in social work training. At this conference Professor A. Marshall generally welcomed the idea of a combined theoretical and practical course: '. . . we not only want practical experience and close contact with reality; we want also that alertness and breadth of mind which are fostered in a greater or less degree by all those studies that are truly of University rank'. At the same time the conference also heard warning notes which still echo in social work education. On the side of the practitioners it was argued that it '. . . would be wiser to keep clear of the Universities, which in social questions were amateurish and academic'. Whilst some of the University teachers argued that 'The part of the University was to inform and train the student's mind and to give him the power of judgment. Principles of action must be acquired elsewhere'.[5]

Despite such misgivings on the part of some university teachers and some social workers the general opinion was in favour of the universities taking an active share in the training of social workers. The School of Social Studies started in Liverpool in 1904, and in 1907 Birmingham established a course of training for social work. Courses on the same lines gradually developed in other universities. The original courses, as we have seen, owed much to the demand from those active in social work. They were also a response to a movement amongst university men, already losing much of its momentum, which supported the greater involvement of the well-educated in the lives of the poor and deprived. This movement owed much to the influence of Jowett and T. H. Green, who were active from the middle of the century. It was their spirit that led Hobhouse, later to become the leading British academic sociologist, to write in 1889: 'I want to see what life and work in London are like. I want to do some social and political work in a very small way, or at any rate come in contact with those who are engaged in it.'[6] But already this spirit of active curiosity was on the wane. As early as 1901 Masterman, an acute observer, noted, 'The Universities and the cultured classes, as a whole, care little about the matter [the problems of modern city life]. The wave of enthusiasm which created the modern settlement has ceased to advance; the buildings remain and a few energetic toilers, and the memory of a great hope.'[7] This observation was repeated by others during the following ten years, and we are forced to the conclusion that social study departments were established in the universities precisely at the time that their most important originating idea had, for a variety of reasons, been exhausted. This is perhaps one of the reasons why the work of these social study departments was in the early years of their existence remarkably undistinguished.

A further reason is to be found in the very difficult task that such departments set themselves. A report by the Joint University Council for Social Studies (representing eleven universities and colleges), in 1918, suggests the main distinctive features of the social study department. It was attempting to establish an identity separate from Law, History and Economics, even though it would need to rely heavily upon some elements in these much longer-established disciplines. Social Study, claimed the report, differed from these other disciplines in, 'Spirit, in method, and in purpose':

> In spirit, because it is distinctly and continuously conscious of the close interconnection of all the several sides of human life in society. In method, because the formal instruction is closely associated with 'practical work', by which is meant the acquiring of a first-hand knowledge of existing social conditions and of personal experience in the working of social institutions. In purpose, because it invites students who have the definite intention to devote themselves to what – with equal indefiniteness but equal intelligibility – is known as social work.

To have a clear idea about the nature of the new departments was admirable, but such clarity in regard to differences from other departments in the university must also have created problems. Some of these problems in relation to social work training are still with us, and they will be discussed later.

Until the end of the Second World War, the two-year diploma courses in social study were the main methods of training for social work, at least as far as the universities were concerned. Courses of training were available outside the university. The Institute of Almoners (now the Institute of Medical Social Workers), ran one such course. There was, however, one exception to the generalization about university courses, namely the Mental Health Course at the London School of Economics. This was started in 1929 as a course for trained and experienced social workers who wished to specialize in social work with the mentally ill. It represented the only professional training (as we would now recognize it), within the university.

The position today is remarkably different and much more complex. This is due to a number of interconnected developments. First, a sharp distinction has come to be made and kept between two stages of educational preparation for social work, the pre-professional and the professional. The two-year social science diploma often tried to combine both stages and succeeded in neither satisfactorily. Second, social administration has developed as an area of study in its own right, so that it is now possible to take a degree in social administration or to study it in some depth, together with such subjects as sociology or psychology. Very recently there has been a development in higher degrees which also confer a professional qualification. There has been a considerable expansion in training available outside the 'normal' social study or social science department. In extra-mural departments, for example, it is now possible to take a number of full-time courses of one or two years' duration. Perhaps the most significant development, certainly in terms of numbers, is the establishment of one-year and two-year training courses outside the university in colleges of further education. In 1967 over 1,200 applicants attempted to obtain a place on the two-year courses. Of these 367 were offered places, so that there are about 3·5 applications for every vacancy on a course. The growth in these courses since they were started in 1963 can be seen in the following table:

Number of Students Awarded the Certificate in Social Work

Year	Two year course	One year course	Total
1963	56	20	76
1964	87	21	108
1965	124	25	149
1966	167	44	211
1967	217	57	274
1968	310*	63*	373*
1969	360*	59*	419*

* Estimated number
(Source: Third Annual Report, CTSW, 1967)

Some idea of the growth in university courses and of the range of provision can be obtained from the following figures for the period 1965/7:

Students completing courses qualifying for the practice of Social Work

One year university courses	1965	1966	1967
Psychiatric Social Work	60	65	70
Child Care	6	6	5
Medical Social Work	8	11	10
General Social Work or Applied Social Studies Course	183	202	235
17 month courses	74	76	70
2 year post-graduate professional courses	—	—	5
4 year integrated courses	—	—	22
Medical Social Work at Institute of MSW	40	45	35
	371	405	452
Probation			
Extra-mural courses	42	68	54
Home Office 1 year specialized course	190	122	116
Child care			
Extra-mural course	35	24	31
Other Educational Establishments	28	56	81
	295	270	282

(Source: Joint University Council for Social and Public Administration)

Provision for social work training has very considerably altered within the present century, and the same can also be said of the content of such training. No historical treatment of this development is so far available, but some of its most important aspects can be grasped from the simple comparison of extracts from two documents, the Confidential Report of the Social Education Committee of the Charity Organization Society submitted in June 1903,[8] and the (Younghusband) Report on Social Workers in the Local Authority Health and Welfare Services, 1959. The first deals with a proposed two-year course of training which would combine, 'lectures and teaching with practical work in the case of students who look forward to fulfilling official duties or serving on Public bodies or undertaking special investigations in social science'. The plan submitted 'takes for granted that a just and well-understood conception of society is a necessary preliminary to good administrative work'. It touches on the various aspects of social science and obligation – the development of society, social economics, some of the problems of social psychology and ethics, such as the formulation of individual and social habit, etc. It includes the history of the development of the industrial classes. It includes also the history and methods of Poor Law relief and charity, especially during the last three centuries. It will be noted that it begins in the first year with lectures on, 'principles directly bearing upon practice', 'concurrently with some practical work'. It starts indeed from the concrete and the practical, and all through keeps in close relation with it. Some idea of the practical work involved can be gained from a synopsis prepared by Mrs Bosanquet,[9] which included:

Study of case-papers and practice in summarizing history of family from running narrative: visiting homes as almoner etc., formation of standard of what a good home should be . . . topography of district . . . industrial conditions of neighbourhood . . . housing and sanitation. . . . Working on Local Government institutions, e.g., as Poor Law Guardians, County Councillors, etc., or promoting the election of desirable candidates.

From this extract we can gain a reasonable picture of the content of the earliest social work training courses. They seem to exhibit a number of characteristics: they are based on the interconnection of fieldwork and academic study; they constitute, in the words of an early social work teacher, *'instruction* in social questions'[10] (italics in original), and they are characterized by a combination of narrow certainty and a wide-ranging curiosity and activity. It may, for example, come as something of a surprise to contemporary advocates of direct social action in social work that their predecessors might have been instructed in 'promoting the election of desirable candidates'. (That such advocates might not have agreed with their predecessors on the criteria of desirability is simply an illustration of the inevitable ambiguity of social action.)

The Younghusband Report, in advocating the establishment of courses of training in social work outside the university, had inevitably to make some statements about the content of such courses. Extracts from the description to be found in the Report can be taken as illustrating some of the most important features of contemporary training. The Report states:

> The courses should be based upon an integration of theory and practice. . . . So far as actual subject matter is concerned, we would regard the purpose of the course as being to give students a good understanding of:
>
> (a) human needs, motivation and behaviour. It is particularly important that students should have a sound general grasp of how human beings function in their physical, psychological and social aspects. . . . It will also be necessary for students to know sufficient about health and disease to recognize, and have some understanding of, variations within the normal as well as deviations, particularly as manifested in mental and physical handicaps, mental illness (neuroses and psychoses), 'problem' family living, and unmarried parenthood:

(b) the social and economic circumstances in which people live including elementary knowledge about the ways in which the national income is made and distributed. . . . The social structure and social attitudes should be primarily studied from the standpoint of different social influences on behaviour, as well as community attitudes towards various forms of handicap and disability:

(c) the social services, statutory and voluntary . . .

The Report continues by suggesting that much of this material may be applied more directly and precisely in the teaching of 'the principles and practice of social work. . . . [This would] include the essential characteristics of social work, as mainly concerned with failures in personal and social functioning, and as it is practised through the methods of casework, groupwork and community organization'.[11]

If we compare this abbreviated description with that given earlier, we can see both continuity and change. Continuity in so far as theory and practice are to be held in the closest relationship, change in both the differentiation of social work method and the expansion of its theoretical basis.

ISSUES AND PROBLEMS

These can conveniently be discussed in terms of the three major roles involved – academic teacher, fieldwork teacher and student.

The academic teacher

To identify the teacher of social work in institutions of higher education as 'academic' is to point to a problem and to invite a vigorous reaction from some of the teachers themselves. 'Academic' is sometimes a word of abuse in this field. Rather we should describe what has to be avoided as a condition of 'academicism'. It would indeed be ridiculous for someone who could be described as an 'academicist', (i.e. preoccupied with the formal and the conventional) to be found in a discipline in which neither form nor convention can be identified with ease. We need a term that distinguishes the 'classroom' teacher from the fieldwork teacher, and for the moment 'academic' seems to suffice.

Part of the difficulty in the terminology reflects the origins of most social work teachers employed as academics. They are often appointed largely on the basis of their own social work experience and practice, and until recently, have thought of themselves as qualified to teach practice rather than the theories that constitute the broad knowledge that social workers should possess. The difficulty with the term 'academic' also stems from the fact that the social work teacher must often feel pulled simultaneously in two different directions. That is, the teacher will want to establish himself or herself within the academic institution, and indeed must do so if the department is to become established and to attract the resources necessary to the work. On the other hand, the students themselves are often outside the institutions as much as, if not more than, they are inside. As we have seen, fieldwork practice occupies a very important part of the course. This means that the academic teacher must be to a greater or lesser degree involved with fieldwork agencies and fieldwork teachers, giving time to husbanding and increasing this valuable resource.

There is also debate about the extent to which social work teachers in an academic setting should become, as it were, clinical teachers. Some feel strongly that the teacher should continue to practice social work concurrently with teaching. The Seebohm Report for example argued that:

> . . . experiments are urgently needed into ways in which individual social work teachers – like teachers in medical schools, for instance – could continue to practise as social workers in social work departments, and as a whole could engage in fieldwork. Social work teaching in both universities and colleges of further education is bound to suffer if social workers who move into teaching must, in

nearly all cases, cease to practise the skills they teach.[12]

As the Report recognized, this suggestion entails many organizational problems and an increase in the number of teachers appointed, but they considered the case very persuasive. There are perhaps two objectives in this proposal that need to be distinguished. First, it could be argued that social work teachers should remain, and be seen to remain, identified with social work. If this was the objective, then, there seemed to be a number of different ways of achieving it. For example, a social work teacher, describing the first year of teaching after a period in social work, has argued that only for some teachers is direct responsibility in the field a necessary means of solving the problem 'to feel and to be seen as a social worker'. Others, however, 'do not feel they need to be actively involved with clients to stay in the main stream of social work':

> They may find that with their teaching commitments their time is fully occupied with research, the development of social work theory, or the activities of professional social work associations. These are vital and useful jobs which involve the people who do them in the current thinking and aims of the social work profession. It is foolish to imagine that those who are occupied in this way are not effective or 'real' social workers, as it is to say that all doctors must always be attending patients to prove their competence as doctors.[13]

Perhaps what is also at stake is the ability to keep teaching 'alive', and we should recognize that there are many different ways of keeping a subject vital.

The second objective may be seen more narrowly; namely, that, as the Seebohm report said, social work teachers are teaching a skill and unless they continue to practise it, they cannot go on teaching it effectively. This seems a convincing argument, but it is also possible to argue that social work skill is more like the skill of the philosopher than the doctor. By this I mean that social work treatment seems very often to be more like 'moral treatment' than medical treatment. The social worker moves in a world of people's reasons for acting, not of viruses causing symptoms. Within this context the practice of social work is concerned with the arguments and the justifications that are met with in everyday life, not with the development of instruments for disclosing the presence of hidden diseases. In this perspective one could adopt some words of Louch originally written in connection with psychology and ethics, and say that what is required in social work, 'is not measurement, experiment, prediction and formal argument, but appraisal, detailed description, reflection and rhetoric . . . the study of action does not require new and hidden events and processes, but reflection upon and re-ordering of what we see men doing'.[14] If this view of social work is adopted, then clearly a social work teacher can practise and rehearse in any situation: his cases are arguments, his tools are words.

So, the social work teacher in an academic situation has to face both outwards to the field from which he has come and inwards towards the institution in which he works. His position is made more difficult because he may not be fully welcomed in either the field or the academic institution. Particularly in the university he may occupy a very marginal position. Within the university, critics will argue that social work is so practical a matter that it is a subject simply for instruction, and as such it has no place in the university. Alternatively, it is so much a question of the subtle nuance of personal relationships plus the downright fortuitous, that it cannot be *taught* at all. In this situation the university teacher has to find an answer to two related questions: what does the university contribute to social work education and what does social work education contribute to university life?

It used to be argued that social training brought the university in contact with what was described as 'real life'. The school of social study, argued one of the earliest teachers in the subject, 'is an amphibious body requiring two elements for its very existence. It belongs to the community as well as to the university and it must have direct contact with administrative bodies of all kinds in the world of action outside.'[15] This contact with the outside world was as valuable to the university as it was necessary to the social study department. Such a view seems to define the university outside 'real life' in a rather arbitrary manner. The idea that social study departments involve contact with agencies 'outside' the university reflects still the present position. The last survey of the work of social study departments showed, for example, a high proportion of staff involved in activities outside the university.[16] Yet we should now be increasingly wary of a firm notion of the boundary between the inside and the outside of the university, and in any event the connection between the university and the outside world are no longer the unique contribution of the social study departments. Indeed they are probably better and more fruitfully maintained in departments such as government. None the less, as we shall see, the study of social work does bring within the orbit of the university a range of problems that could provide material for research and continuous reflection.

The strongest case against a place for social work in the university is a general case that would nullify the claims of a number of another studies, like social administration, engineering and so on. This is the argument that the university should be concerned with helping students to speak a language which is explanatory.[17] What is useful, what is vocational has no place in a university. It should be granted at once that social work education has often in the past been both highly vocational and of a rather poor quality. Yet this is not necessarily the case. It could be argued that a liberalized social work education has a legitimate place in the university. First, however, it would be necessary to show what a liberalized social work education would be like, what it would resemble. Pursuing this line of argument it is necessary to note the different ways in which we refer to a liberal education. Peters[18] has distinguished the following meanings. When we say that a vocational training should be liberalized we could be making at least three distinct proposals. We could be suggesting that people should be taught in such a way that stress was laid not on the end product, but on the value of the activities that somehow went to make the final product. Thus, cooking could be taught so that the consumer value of the product was less emphasized than the standards involved in the various constituent activities. Alternatively, practical interests could be used as starting points for voyages into territory surrounding the vocational activity. Thus, medicine could be taught as the historical cumulation of past experience, and the student would be encouraged to study past practice not simply as a dead technique, but as a way of solving a problem that was connected to other ways of solving problems available at that time and in that society. Lastly, a vocational education could be said to be liberal if the knowledge required was not taught in a dogmatic way.

Now social work education has in its comparatively short life suffered from teachers who were diffident dogmatists, but this is the least important sense in which social work education needs to be liberalized. It is in the first and second sense mentioned above that social work education could become much more liberal than it is at present. If it were liberalized in these ways, then it could be argued with some plausibility, that it presented a range of interesting intellectual problems appropriate to and offering advantage to university life. Basically what is being studied in social work education is human action within a number of different perspectives. At many points the student takes up again and presses forward to a new understanding an aspect of historical, literary and scientific pursuits previously abandoned as a dead letter or accepted as 'settled'. Two brief illustrations may help to clarify this statement. They concern some aspects of judgment in social work, and some elements of the problem of describing and understanding human behaviour.

The social worker is continuously making judgments about people – about the depth of feeling they are experiencing, the kind of people they are, the significance of changes in behaviour, and so on. Judgments of this kind, (which are clearly distinguishable from the expression of any kind of condemnatory attitude) seem to call for a blending of intellectual and emotional operations that are equally demanded by judgments about the literary quality of, say, a novel or a poem. The new element in the situation seems to be contained in the fact that the social worker has to act upon his judgment within the context of particular relationships, both with the client and with his colleagues. It seems also to be the case that, in making such judgments, the social worker is especially likely to stress the emotional component at the expense of the intellectual. Taylor has recently suggested that this danger is also to be found in teacher training and his quotation from Hofstadter's book on anti-intellectualism applies equally to social work education:

> Intellect is pitted against feeling, on the ground that it is somehow inconsistent with warm emotion. It is pitted against character because it is widely believed that intellect stands for mere cleverness, which transmutes easily into the sly or the diabolical. It is pitted against practicality, since theory is held to be opposed to practice, and the 'purely' theoretical mind is so much disesteemed. It is pitted against democracy, since intellect is thought to be a form of distinction that defies egalitarianism.[19]

Yet, in applying such a diagnosis to social work and social work education, it is important to recognize its tendency to swing too far in the support of 'intellect'. It is the blending of rational and emotional elements that is required for a social work judgment. In the exploration of this mixture of elements the social work student will begin to see the ways in which intellectual confusion and emotional muddle and uncertainty reflect each other.

But on what subject matter is the judgment exercised? If the social worker wishes to describe and evaluate human behaviour, is he simply describing and judging what he sees or is there an unavoidable value element intermingled with his description? This sounds like the familiar distinction between 'is' and 'ought' statements and the impossibility of deducing from a description of what is the case any statement about what ought to be. This, judging by the many references in social work commentary, seems to be a settled question, something that is taken as a doctrine and observed rigidly. Yet within the context of social work action we meet both the old division between 'is' and 'ought' and also certain bridge notions which carry traffic between the two positions, even though the style of transportation could not be described as deductive. Ideas like those of 'need' seem to serve as a kind of link, and 'need' is certainly a notion that receives emphasis in social work writing, whether it is concerned with large questions concerning public provision, (child care needs) or with understanding particular behaviour, ('it seems he needs to have an unfaithful wife'). 'Need' is often used somewhat spuriously to convey an impression of access to knowledge hidden from others when social workers simply insert 'need' before any description of behaviour, (the client steals = he needs to steal) but this vulgarized usage does not destroy more legitimate use. But even when the term is being used helpfully, how helpful is it in the description and evaluation of behaviour? This question can partly be answered by reference to the study of actual societies, and by making such references we see the social worker moving in a most interesting way between conceptual and empirical enquiry. Take, for example, the following comment on the significance of eating amongst the Arapesh people:

[Eating] is not a distinct act satisfying a single need. Food to the Arapesh is good; it incorporates intensive social intercourse; it is the medium of intimacy and identification with others, the symbol of human relations which to them are the primary good. It satisfies the total individual. When we analyse the mouthful of yams into so much nutrition plus so much social warmth. . . . we do not find these distinctions or elements – we create them.[20]

The students

Of the problems facing the social work student three have been selected as of major importance. They arise from three connected questions that the student must often ask himself: What kind of course is a social work education course? What strains does it impose? What shall I be equipped to do at the end of the course?

The student, applying for a course of social work education is applying to study a subject and to join a profession that has never enjoyed high status. A study by the Council of Europe stated: 'The observations made . . . about the inadequate status of the social worker are unanimous. The social worker undergoes a long and intensive training and carries out a highly responsible job but, generally speaking, receives neither fitting recognition nor suitable pay. . . .'[21] The comparatively low status of social work is partly due to the fact that social work has for some time been a predominantly female profession, a fact that male aspirants must consider in all its implications. This situation, however, is changing. A study of over 2,700 first-year students in Canada and America found that in 1960 41 per cent were men; this compared with about 12 per cent between 1931 and 1933 and 34 per cent between 1953 and 1955.[22] (It also appears that men are more attracted to certain types of social work, i.e. to community work rather than social casework.) Fewer students in the study had parents who were social workers than students of other professions with fathers in the same field, and whilst parents, relatives and teachers did not oppose the choice of social work as a career, only about half the students reported that their choice was approved. Some indication of the range of parental reaction can be obtained from another study[23] which investigated parental attitudes to the prospect of children becoming social workers.

On most courses, students face the problem of concurrent field and academic work. This means a change in the focus of work and also quite often a tension between demands, i.e., to write an essay and to record the fieldwork for supervision. They are also introduced to a range of theory from which they must choose and make some working synthesis or to an already synthesized approach which they must learn and accept or reject. The use of theory is a particularly difficult and crucial issue and Stevenson has recently suggested that it involves two stages: '(1) The ability constructively to discuss theory in relation to practice and to see the relevance of each to the other. This involves a capacity to transfer and to generalize. (2) The ability to *use* theory in practice; to develop skill by the application of theory.'[24] This formulation, suggesting that theory has a direct relationship with the development of skill, raises another problem for the student, namely, what relationship is expected to exist between the various theories that he is taught and his practical activity. It is far from clear that skill is increased by the application of theory. As Louch has suggested:

> If a baseball player wishes to improve his batting average, he does not go to the physicist whose laws govern what happens when a bat hits a ball, or to the physiologist, whose expertise entitles him to say something about the movements of his muscles as responses to the stimuli acting upon his eye. He goes instead, to the batting coach who, though entirely ignorant of these theories, has the long observation and practice which enable him to diagnose the batter's particular difficulties. It is like this in clinical practice.[25]

As we have seen, the student is presented with a wide range of theoretical ideas and it is not always clear what relevance they have to practice. The student is further hampered by the fact that the literature of social work itself is essentially non-cumulative, and exhortatory. Whilst articles refer at considerable length to other social work writing, they do so in a way that is decorative rather than useful. There is very little idea of slowly developing ideas that can be grouped together as a school or of the recognition that one particular idea or finding is inconsistent with findings already accepted, if not well established.

These are some of the difficulties for the student, but they also, of course, constitute a challenge. This challenging character is also evident when we turn to the personal difficulties that students experience. As one of them stated: 'I had very little clear notion of what I expected the course to be like before I started on it. I do recall, however, that I was expecting to feel "steamrollered" at the end. I did.' Students often have very high expectations of their social work course; that it may transform them personally or give them a set of receipts for instant success in social work. In other words, the course is seen as a kind of therapy or a way of obtaining a set of rules. Both expectations are due for disappointments. Indeed they must be disappointed. Part of the personal problem aspect stems from what has already been said: people will react to the strains, e.g., of split practical and academic work, in different ways. There are, also, other sources for personal strain. The students are putting to the test their convictions that they can help others. As they study in some detail their actual interaction with others, they begin to see that some or a great deal of what they do and say may not be helpful, that they do not – for a variety of reasons – actually like everyone they meet as clients. The problems that people present appear to be much more complex than might at first sight have appeared to be the case, and the student has to try to help people behaving in ways of which he strongly disapproves – parents ill-treating their children, husbands attempting to drive their wives mad, members of a group 'scapegoating' one of their number, people accepting or justifying repressive social arrangements. In the face of these and other troubles, the social work student may experience a number of stages of personal adaptation. These have been described by Reynolds in the following terms: '. . . acute consciousness of self, sink-or-swim adaptation, understanding the situation without power to control one's acting on it, relative mastery'.[26] As he goes through the course the student is experiencing most of the strains and uncertainties that characterize the profession he is about to enter. Wilson[27] has described the role of the teacher, and the role conflicts and insecurities that he delineated resemble closely those of the social worker. It should, however, be noted that this description is not derived from or tested by systematic empirical observation. This remains an important task for the future in many professions.

Wilson outlines a number of conflicts and insecurities. First, there are no clear lines of demarcation whereby the teacher, (or social worker or, one might add, priest) knows when he has done his job; when he can rest contented that he has done as much as could be expected, when he can feel he has achieved the aims of his job. Nokes has commented in this respect on the frequency of a 'marked reaction of distaste to the introduction into the welfare professions of concepts of *efficiency*':

> It is usual to find practitioners justifying their work not in terms of any known degree of efficiency in the pursuit of a given goal, but in terms of the 'personal satisfaction' that accrues to those who give themselves in this way. . . . A 'good day' therefore tends to be one on which the practitioner 'did a good day's work'. It is not necessarily a day on which some outstanding degree of objective 'good was done'.[28]

There is in addition a difficulty for the teacher, (and the social worker) in being both a disciplinary agent and an affective agent. The 'control' function of social work has recently been re-emphasized, and some social workers find this more acceptable than others. It is possible that the tension can be resolved by thinking of the time dimension in social work help – beginning with affective interaction on the client's terms and ending with acceptance by the client of control and discipline, perhaps self-control. Others will find this kind of resolution illusory.

Second, both teachers and social workers in the course of and by the nature of their work are brought into contact with a wide range of people who have opinions, often strongly held, about what the professional task should be. Social workers have to establish working relationships with administrators at various levels, with doctors, teachers, clients, and so on. In this situation conflict is likely to arise between the different prescriptions offered for the task and between any of these and the professional's own view of what ought to be done. Thus, in the fostering situations the foster father may believe that the child care officer should help his wife with 'all the forms and things; help her to get the best out of the council' (the child care officer should not be concerned with 'private' affairs of the foster home). The foster mother, on the other hand, may see the social worker's main task as the giving of expert advice on the handling of the child's behaviour when this becomes difficult (a limited concern with 'private' matters is desirable). The foster child may see the child care officer as 'his' worker who should be the main link with his own home and his main hope for the future, (the social worker should be concerned with the child's 'private' affairs).

Finally, insecurity often arises because of the social worker's marginal position. This marginality has a number of different aspects. The social worker often occupies a marginal position in regard to his or her clients. By this I mean that social work intervention is unlikely to be influential unless it can make alliance with the most powerful forces and the most important objectives in that major part of the client's life that lies, as it were, 'outside' the social work interview. The social worker's position is also marginal in the sense that time spent at 'the client face' is likely to be comparatively short, taking into account the social worker's total career; promotion tends to remove the social worker from direct contact with clients. Marginality also refers to the position of social workers in particular organizations and from the point of view of the wider society. Thus, in such organizations as hospitals, prisons, and so on, the withdrawal of social workers would in no visible sense threaten the continued existence of the organization. In such organizations, as in the wider society, the social worker often seems to stand for activities and objectives which are not of major interest or importance. As Wilson had stated of the teacher, 'The teacher has been described as someone who expresses value-consensus. The conflict of his role is clear in a society where such consensus is no longer a reality.'[29]

THE FIELDWORK TEACHER

The fieldwork teacher is currently in great demand. It is frequently asserted that major expansion in the training programme is hindered by the lack of suitable social workers who could take on the task of fieldwork instruction. It has been calculated that in the year October 1962 to September 1963, over 1,500 fieldwork placements (of at least four weeks) were provided for nearly 1,000 students from a total of 40 courses of professional social work training.[30] It is likely that most of the students were placed singly, not in groups: on Certificate in Social Work Courses 1965/6, 67 per cent of all students were placed singly and 73 per cent of field-work teachers had only one student at a time. In the majority of these situations the fieldworker will be taking on an important educational task in addition to his or her own work. A time study of fieldwork teaching in the field of child care found that, over the first six weeks of the student's period in the department, the majority of supervisors spent between 16 and 21 hours. This time was divided between the different activities that together constitute fieldwork supervision – finding suitable cases, discussion with the student, (both informal and in the supervisory conference), preparation, reading of the student's records, discussion with the academic staff concerned, and work on cases carried by the student.[31]

The educational task of the fieldwork teacher is not only time-consuming it is also complex, partly through the relationships entailed and partly because of the content of the fieldwork course. These two subjects are of major importance and the following discussion will refer only to selected aspects, but, it is hoped, in a way that illuminates the more general problems.

The fieldwork teacher simply by virtue of assuming this role enters a number of relationships which are difficult if challenging. First, she enters a special kind of relationship with colleagues: she assumes a bridge position between her agency and the academic centre. Such a position is hard to hold, since the fieldwork teacher must, if she is to provide a meaningful experience for the student, remain identified with the field and with her agency in particular. On the other hand, she must have more sympathy with the educational objectives of the academic centre. This may be difficult in view of current myths and ideas about the nature of education at such centres. The kind of difficulty I have in mind can be illustrated from the field of education. Taylor in discussing the relationship between the staff of the teacher training college and the teacher in the field, comments:

A frequent and familiar criticism is that the staff of the college have an excessive concern with theory, and there is a measure of resentment among teachers at the good fortune of those colleagues who have escaped into apparently less arduous and demanding work. Another source of difficulty derives from the inability of anyone outside the classroom situation to appreciate the importance of say today's 'system maintenance' for the practising teacher. Once out of the classroom the lecturer or administrator becomes subject to new and different sets of institutional pressures and demands, and it is not easy to enter fully into the kinds of situational pressure to which the teacher is subject.[32]

These and similar difficulties are exactly paralleled in the field of social work education.

Second, of course, the fieldwork teacher has to form relationships with his or her students. Such relationships are likely to be complex partly because one of the assumptions in social work education is that, as far as possible, the student's learning experiences should be tailored to his (changing) educational needs. It is complex also because of the three main elements in the relationship. The supervisor is a teacher, and a helper, and someone who carries administrative responsibility within the agency. As teacher the supervisor has to try to select those learning experiences that will most easily provide educational opportunities for the particular student: as helper the supervisor should attempt to facilitate the student's grasp of these experiences, but in ways that do involve him (or her) in a 'treatment' role in relation to the student. Yet the agency in which the supervisor works does not exist only to help in the training of social workers, and the work of the student must, for administrative as well as educational reasons, not be allowed to fall below the bare minimum of competence. Thus, as administrator and as teacher the fieldwork supervisor would be concerned at a student's failure to follow through certain important organizational implications of the work.

It is frequently stated that 'the supervisor is the teacher who is responsible for giving the student a "course" in field-work'.[33] This raises the question of the possible content of such a course, assuming that it will in major respects tailor to individual needs. One way of approaching this question is to consider the kinds of judgment required at the end of a period of fieldwork. If we can see the kinds of matter on which a fieldwork teacher is asked to pass judgment, then it should be possible to see something of the content of what he or she teaches.

Social work objectives are characteristically described in the widest possible terms – to promote mental health, to prevent all known social ills, etc. With this kind of end in view – if indeed such ends can ever be 'in view' – it is extremely difficult for the social worker to know when he is doing well in his work, and this means that it is equally difficult to know at the end of a period of fieldwork whether the student has attained the necessary minimum level of professional competence. Increasing attention is being paid to this problem, and a number of informed attempts have been made to specify in some detail the requirements necessary before qualification. The following would represent some of the main aspects covered:

Use of supervision

The fieldwork teacher will consider the extent to which the student comes prepared for the supervisory session and is able to learn. It would be important to assess the extent to which the student can appraise the understanding he has gained and the gaps that remain in his knowledge and the weaknesses in his developing skill. In particular the supervisor will attend to the extent to which the student attempts to use his theoretical knowledge in the practical situation and the way in which he does so. Finally, the supervisor will need to assess the way in which the student relates to the supervisor and deals with the elements of dependence and hostility that may well arise.

This very brief description raises at once two important questions. First, we are dealing very much in terms of judgments rather than measurements. The fieldwork teacher will obviously seek to base a judgment on evidence, but the result of her judgment may well be a description of the ways in which a student works. Some descriptions will be incompatible with the description of a qualified social worker, but no numerical value can be assigned. Second, it is not clear how far 'the use of supervision' represents an area on which evidence will be sought for other matters, e.g., the way in which the student relates to clients rather than a sub-subject as it were, in which the student had to pass.

Behaviour in the agency

Obviously all the relevant behaviour is within the agency, but in assessing the student we should try to avoid a global judgment and concentrate instead on as many aspects of his activity as can be meaningfully separated. In this section reference is made to activity outside that in the face-to-face situation with clients or other relevant groups. The student should in this context have reasonably good working relationships with colleagues, and be able to organize his work so that, e.g., he uses facilities, (such as typing, etc.)

appropriately. He has often to contact other agencies from his temporary 'base'. When he does so, he should be able to present the policies and activities of his own agency clearly. He should have faced and settled such problems as: the behaviour expected of me in the agency is 'unnatural' to me; I am being 'moulded' to the shape required by the agency. He should feel able to question agency policy constructively, and to appreciate that different personalities and different ways of working can often be contained within any organization, and can achieve results. Ability to record appropriately and in different ways is important.

Behaviour with clients

The student should be able to listen both to what is being said and to what the client or clients are trying to tell him. He should be able to report this clearly and then to assess the significance of the observations in one meeting to an overall pattern that seems to make sense of the 'case'. Reliability in the obvious sense of keeping appointments is essential, but so is being psychologically available and consistently trying to understand. In dealing with individuals or groups, a student should be able to refer when necessary to the relationship between client and worker and to the ways in which past and present relationships are affecting the problem and attempts at its resolution. Social workers should be able to allow and sometimes encourage the expression of feelings that are about to be expressed, whether these are hostile or positive. They should not be afraid to ask questions, but show discernment of of when not to, and what questions to ask. The student should be able to recognize those situations in which he is likely to get very anxious and to have developed some way of coping with these. He should have dealt with some of the authority aspects of his work and be able to use knowledge of social services. He should be able to handle beginnings and endings of contacts, and have a good idea of what professional conduct is and some sense of his own value as a professional person.

The fact that the fieldwork teacher may be required to pass opinions on these aspects of the student's work indicates the boundaries of a course in fieldwork. It is clearly a difficult and complex course, open to distortion and error of several kinds. Both academic and fieldwork teachers must recognize their considerable power in the situation. They can, without too much difficulty, inculcate and transmit an unreliable orthodoxy and an uncritical acceptance of the present, which provides no basis on which to meet the changing needs and demands of the future. Alternatively, they can provide no guidance at all, beyond the attachment, promiscuous and slight, to whatever fashion currently prevails.

NOTES

[1] Bosanquet, S. R., op. cit.
[2] Addams, J., *Philanthropy and Social Progress*, New York, 1893.
[3] ibid.
[4] Bosanquet, H., 'Methods of Training', C.O.S. Occasional Papers Third Series, Paper No. 3.
[5] See-Smith, M., *Professional Education for Social Work in Britain*, Family Welfare Association, 1952.
[6] From a letter quoted in Hobson, J. A., and Ginsberg, M., *L. T. Hobhouse*, Allen and Unwin, 1931, p. 26.
[7] Masterman, C. F., *The Heart of the Empire*, 1901, p. 35.
[8] To be found in Appendix III in See-Smith, op. cit.
[9] ibid.
[10] Macadam, E., 'The Universities and The Training of the Social Worker', *Hibbert Journal*, XII, 1914.
[11] Younghusband *Report*, para. 891.
[12] Report of the (Seebohm) Committee.
[13] Cheetham, J., 'From Social Work to Teaching', *Case Conference*, XIV, No. 8, December 1967.
[14] Louch, A. R., *Explanation and Human Action*, London: Blackwell, 1966, p. 235.
[15] Macadam, E., *The Social Servant in the Making*, London: Allen & Unwin, 1945, p. 128.
[16] Jones, K., *The Teaching of Social Studies in British Universities*, Occasional Papers on Social Administration No. 12, 1964, p. 52.
[17] See, e.g., Cowling, M., *The Nature and Limits of Political Science*, London: Oxford University Press, 1963.

[18] Peters, R., *Ethics and Education*, London: Allen & Unwin, 1966.

[19] Hofstadter, R., *Anti-Intellectualism in American Life*, quoted in Taylor, W., *Society and the Education of Teachers*, London: Faber, 1969, p. 278.

[20] Lee, D., *Freedom and Culture*, New York: Prentice-Hall, 1959.

[21] *Social Workers, Role, Training and Status*, Social Committee of the Council of Europe, Strasbourg, 1967.

[22] Pims, A., *Who Chooses Social Work, When and Why?*, Council on Social Work Education, U.S.A., 1963.

[23] Unkovic, C., 'The Image of Social Work is Changing', *Case Conference*, May, 1966.

[24] Stevenson, O., 'Problems in the Use of Theory in Social Work Education', *British Journal of Psychiatric Social Work*, IX, 1, 1967.

[25] *Louch, A. R.*, op. cit.

[26] Reynolds, B., *Learning and Teaching in the Practice of Social Work*, New York: Russell & Russell, 1965.

[27] Wilson, B., 'The Teacher's Role – A Sociological Analysis', *British Journal of Sociology*, March 1962.

[28] Nokes, P., *The Professional Task in Welfare Practice*, London: Routledge & Kegan Paul, 1967, p. 25.

[29] Wilson, B., op. cit.

[30] Clement Brown, S., and Gloyne, E., *The Field Training of Social Workers*, London: Allen & Unwin, 1966, p. 43.

[31] Timms, N., 'Time Study of Supervision', *Case Conference*, July, 1962.

[32] Taylor, W., op. cit.

[33] Young, P., *The Student and Supervision in Social Work Education*, London: Routledge & Kegan Paul, 1967, p. 13.

Subject Index

Author Index